Go Quickly and Tell

Go Quickly
and Tell

edited by Janet Sugioka

The Bethany Press
St. Louis, Missouri

© 1973 by The Bethany Press

Library of Congress Cataloging in Publication Data

Main entry under title:

Go quickly and tell.

    1. Devotional calendars. I. Sugioka, Janet,
1913–   ed.
BV4810.G53   242'.2   73-15628
ISBN 0-8272-1215-1

Scripture quotations marked "RSV" are from the *Revised Standard Version of the Bible*, copyrighted 1946 and 1952 by the Division of Christian Education, National Council of the Churches of Christ in the U.S.A., and used by permission.

Quotations marked "Phillips" are from *The New Testament in Modern English*, revised edition. Trans. by J. B. Phillips. Copyright © J. B. Phillips 1958, 1960, 1972. Used by permission of Macmillan Publishing Co., New York, and Collins Publishers, London.

The quotation marked "Amplified Bible" is from *The Amplified Bible, Old Testament, Part II.* Copyright © 1964 by Zondervan Publishing House, Grand Rapids, Michigan. Used by permission of the publisher.

Quotations marked "Living Bible" are from *The Living Bible, Paraphrased.* Copyright © 1971 by Tyndale House Publishers, Wheaton, Illinois. Used by permission of the publisher.

Quotations marked "Moffatt" are from *The Bible: A New Translation* by James Moffatt. Copyright 1954 by James A. R. Moffatt. Reprinted by permission of Harper & Row, Publishers, Inc., New York, and Hodder & Stoughton, London.

Quotations marked "NEB" are from *The New English Bible, New Testament.* © The Delegates of the Oxford University Press and The Syndics of the Cambridge University Press 1961. Reprinted by permission.

Quotations marked "TEV" are from the *Today's English Version of the New Testament*, copyright © American Bible Society 1966, 1971; or from The Psalms for Modern Man in the Today's English Version, copyright American Bible Society 1970. Used by permission.

Quotations marked "KJV" are from the *King James Version of the Bible.*

The photographs are from Religious News Service and are used by permission.

Distributed by The G. R. Welch Company, Toronto, Ontario, Canada.

MANUFACTURED IN THE UNITED STATES OF AMERICA

Contents

Another Devotional Book! Why?	7
Editor's Note	9
In the Beginning	11
Bread	13
Quiet Times Are Important	17
Gratitude	20
In the World but Not of the World	24
Advent Begins	27
The Meaning of the Family Today	32
The Essence of My Faith	35
Christmas	39
Begin	43
Youth and the Open Door	47
Run to the Cry	50
Spiritual Succotash	54
God Is!	57
Peace	61
The Christian Faith	65
Listening	69
Lent Begins	72
The Miracle of Healing	77
Available Power	80
Reaching Out	84
Known by Their Fruits	87
Growing	91
We Know the Words . . . Give Us Lives to Match	94
Easter	98
Finding God	102
Reconciliation—How Do You Spell It?	106
Recipe for Love	110
Family Relationships	114
Becoming a Sensitive Christian	117
Varieties of Service but the Same Lord	121
Saying "Yes" to Self Brings Life	124
I Am the Vine; You Are the Branches	129
This Is the Day	132

God Is! Rejoice!	136
Human Liberation	139
Personal Relations	144
Ways of Loving	147
The Worth of Each Person	151
Salvation Today	154
Bodies of Water I Have Known	159
Practicing the Presence of God	162
Road Signs of Life	166
Grace	169
Love	173
A Life of Service	177
Two Minutes to God	181
The Fruit of the Spirit	184
Creation	189
Keeping Things in Perspective	192
Spiritual Availability	196
Commitment	199
Looking to the Future	203
Eternal, Yet Always New	206
Index of Authors	207

Another Devotional Book! Why?

To plan for a celebration of the one hundredth anniversary of the organized work of women of the Christian Church (Disciples of Christ), the Advisory Council of the Department of Christian Women's Fellowship appointed a centennial committee. The members were Edna Brown, June Christensen, Betty Fiers, Lorraine Lollis, Connie Shannon, Helen F. Spaulding, ex officio, and Jessie M. Trout, chairman.

From the first meeting, held in March, 1971, the committee decided that we should not linger in the past. But who can forget the courage of Mrs. Caroline Neville Pearre? As she rose from her morning devotions on April 10, 1874, after praying for a leader to organize the women for missionary work, a thought that seemed almost like a voice came to her: "Why can't you do it?" "I will," she answered and began immediately.

She wrote to Thomas Munnell, corresponding secretary of the American Christian Missionary Society, who had suggested that the church might get on with its defunct missionary enterprise if it committed it to "the sisters of some of our states." His reply has illuminated and inspired the hearts of each succeeding generation of women leaders. He wrote, "This is a flame of the Lord's kindling, and no man can extinguish it."

Mrs. Pearre went to the General Missionary Convention in Cincinnati in October, 1874, and led the women in the organization of the Christian Woman's Board of Missions. Before long the CWBM, as it came to be known, supported overseas missions and home missions, led in some innovations in Christian education, and in general areas aided the program of the total church.

But what of our todays and tomorrows? The century has brought many changes. The new organization became international sometime about its tenth birthday, when Canadian women linked their budding organization with the CWBM. For the past twenty years, women's work has been maintained as the Department of Christian Women's Fellowship in The United Christian Missionary Society. Now this department enters the centennial celebration with a new title. The Department of Church Women in the Division of Homeland Ministries will continue to serve Christian Women's Fellowships in local churches and, in addition, will serve women in such other ways as the new day demands.

Who is bold enough to predict the future? An old hymn says, "Change and decay in all around I see." Change? Yes. It is inevitable and perhaps it will be quicker and more dramatic than we can imagine. But decay? No, not if we build on the spiritual foundation and the great structure of cooperation and unity that we have inherited.

What, the committee wondered, should be the lodestar of our celebration that will guide us today and plumb the measure of tomorrow? We decided to publish a devotional book written by women from our own ranks. This book, *Go Quickly and Tell*, is by us and for us. May it quicken our gratitude for past blessings and guide us in prayer for living wisdom for today and courageous creativeness for the future. The first lines of Psalm 67, known as our missionary benediction through the years, seem just right for today's celebration and tomorrow's expectancy. "God be merciful unto us, and bless us; and cause his face to shine upon us; that thy way may be known upon earth, thy saving health among all nations." (Psalm 67:1−2, KJV.)

Jessie M. Trout, Owen Sound, Ontario, Canada

Editor's Note

When the members of the centennial committee suggested the title for this book, they were thinking of the Easter story told in chapter 28 of Matthew. An angel at the empty tomb reassured the women who came to mourn, urging them to go quickly and tell the disciples the great news of the Resurrection.

The women of the Christian Church (Disciples of Christ) in the U.S.A. and Canada who contributed to this book were asked to share with us—drawing from the experience, thought, and strength of their own lives—some of their deepest personal insights about God and people. Thus they join the long line of women—stretching back not just a hundred but nearly two thousand years—who have hastened to tell, in word, gesture, presence, and action, the Good News of God with us now and always.

These meditations were written from the heart. They should be read from the heart, with the absorbed attention that is a form of prayer and with an openness to new ways of perceiving reality.

It has been a joy to work with the writers; with Rosemary Roberts, associate executive secretary of the Department of Church Women; with the DCW staff; and with Jeanette Kampen and Dorothy Eicks, former assistant editors of The Bethany Press. May the Spirit of creative love speak through it to us all.

In the Beginning • November 1–3

LISTENING

November 1

Psalms 46:10a

In 1874 an idea that produced action was born as a great woman "listened." Out of Caroline Neville Pearre's *silences* came the knowledge of what she was to do. Every woman in the Christian Church should own and read the book by Lorraine Lollis, *The Shape of Adam's Rib* (Bethany Press). It tells of women who wisely met the needs of their day and projected programs for the future because the journey inward had given them the wisdom and courage for such a task. No responsibility is too great for a Christian woman when she believes that what has been decided for action is God's will. We become confident as we learn the art of listening for God's direction. To read *Search for Silence*, by Elizabeth O'Connor (Word Books), is an exciting adventure for one who needs help in the art of listening.

WISDOM

November 2

Eternal God, we remember the words about our Lord—"And Jesus increased in wisdom . . ." (Luke 2:52a, RSV). We know that often we are governed by emotion rather than by objective thinking. Help us remember that the early leaders of our movement believed they should do more than serve dinners, wash dishes, and be "pastors' helpers." If they were to give as much for others as for themselves, if they were to help send committed people to share the message, they must know geography and sound financial procedures as well as the Bible. Those women began to study, plan, and make decisions. Thus they developed wisdom as well as devotion.

Our Father, give us the wisdom we need in this chaotic and troubled world, in the name of Jesus Christ. Amen.

COURAGE
November 3

"You have a certain grasp of the basis of true knowledge. You have without doubt very great advantages. But, prepared as you are to instruct others, do you ever teach yourself anything?" (Rom. 2:20—21, Phillips.)

This is one of the most penetrating confrontations in the New Testament. It takes courage to face our own inadequacies before we swing into action in Christian service. Whatever qualities our early leaders lacked, they had courage. Do we have such courage today? Are we sure of what we believe? Are we tempted just to keep the organization going, rather than to discover the gifts of women and release them to serve with joy? Do we have what it takes to really witness, no matter what the cost?

Mossie Allman Wyker, Berea, Kentucky

Bread ● November 4—10

November 4

"I wouldn't think I was home if I didn't smell bread baking on Saturdays." The delicious aroma of freshly baked bread spelled home, warmth, love, and security to the young university student, visiting his parents for the weekend.

To the children of Israel the bread of Egypt was sustenance; the manna in the desert was sustenance. To Christ bread was a symbol of life, of fellowship, of sacrifice. To the early Christians it represented sharing the body of Christ. To the peoples of the world today it represents food—or the lack of it.

An element so basic, so essential, so ordinary can bring inspiration and depth to our thoughts and draw us near to God, our Provider, Sustainer, Guide, and Savior.

BROKEN BREAD

November 5
1 Cor. 11:23

The common meal in Asia is a way of expressing close association among participants. Thus it was expected that the meal in the Upper Room would have deep emotional overtones. To share the bread was also expected. Even the farewell. But for the broken bread to represent Jesus' body? And to give thanks in the face of death?

When Jesus walked directly into the hands of his betrayers, he knew that even though the giving of his life meant liberation, death would have the same agony for him as for any other human being.

When the disciples accepted the fragment of broken bread, they committed themselves to share this suffering.

Break and hold a fragment of bread just now . . .

Jesus said, "Are ye able . . . ?" (Matt. 20:22, KJV.)

A PIECE OF BREAD

November 6

Hold a piece of bread in your hand.
- —It represents basic food, an essential to life.
- —People have died for want of bread.
- —People have stolen for need of bread.
- —Bread has been shared and new relationships formed.
- —Bread has been wasted while the world has been in need. Jesus said, "I am the bread of life . . . come down from heaven" (John 6:35a, 38a, NEB).

Think of the Bread of Life . . .
- —It represents food for the soul, essential to life.
- —People have found new life through the Bread.
- —This Bread is ours for the asking and the taking.
- —The Bread of Life offers us abundant living, freedom, and eternal life.

ONE LOAF OF BREAD
November 7

The loaf of bread was placed on a stone in the center of our circle. It was golden brown and crispy.

Our purpose at the CWF retreat that morning was to celebrate God's love at Communion. With the warm glow of friendship, the bright sun, the beautiful lakeside, the fresh loaf of bread, we heard the words, "Because there is one loaf, we, many as we are, are one body, for it is one loaf of which we all partake" (1 Cor. 10:17, NEB).

We, all different, one loaf? We, like bread, essential to all people? We, like the particles of the loaf, essential to one another? Possibly in this setting we could accept that fact. But out there in the world?

O God, let our oneness in you show your likeness to the world. Send us forth to reflect the love of Christ.

NEED FOR BREAD
November 8

The sandwich fell by the roadside. The loud voice of an angry child rudely invaded the village quiet. On her way to school, she had looked at the lunch prepared for her. Not the kind of sandwich she liked, so she threw it away. My first thought was of the litter, then of the waste, then of the ingratitude. Bread earned by the labor of her family—the sandwich made by thoughtful hands.

But the angry gesture was a cry of need for a deeper thing. Most significant to life is the need not for physical food but for spiritual food. The "redeemed" whose whole being is tuned to the love of Christ is the one who appreciates love and the opportunity to love.

Jesus said, 'Scripture says, "man cannot live on bread alone; he lives on every word that God utters,"' (Matt. 4:4, NEB).

OUR DAILY BREAD
November 9

The happy sound of children laughing comes over the radio waves. The announcer says, "Bring along the Ben's—nature's bounty in a bag." There is no question whether there is any "Ben's" (bread), or enough. No question about the cost—just the fact that we can package "nature's bounty" so that we may take it wherever we go.

A well-known Canadian TV personality repeatedly tells us that he got "turned off on God" when he saw the starving masses in India. It is a sobering fact that the Lord's table is spread mostly to the children of God who are well- (or over-) fed. But the prayer, "Give us this day *our* daily bread" is a petition that *all* may be fed.

However will they be fed unless the redeemed of the world are willing to share?

HOW MUCH BREAD?
November 10

"How much gas?" asked the attendant. "How much bread we got, baby?" asked the youth of the girl in the battered car. Then to the attendant, "Okay, man, fill 'er up."

Our need for regular bodily sustenance has been so generally referred to as "daily bread" that the youth of our day have transferred the term to mean currency. Daily bread can also remind us of our need for spiritual food. Abundant spiritual bread is available through Christ so that we may always be satisfied, filled. When life is demanding, when problems descend with seemingly unbearable pressure, Christ is always present to uphold us.

Jesus said, "Whoever comes to me shall never be hungry..." (John 6:35a, NEB).

How much bread we got . . . ?

Jean Gordon, Milton, Nova Scotia, Canada

Quiet Times Are Important • November 11–17

November 11

" 'Be still, and know that I am God.' " (Psalm 46:10, RSV).

This sounds like such an easy way to know God, and yet sometimes I feel it is the hardest way.

We seldom take a quiet moment to listen and hear his directions. We often seem too busy going nowhere to really put our minds at rest in God.

We do find God sometimes in the quiet places of our lives—in the beauty of a flower, the wonder of a lush meadow, the laughter of a child, the smile of a friend. But do we stop and listen to what God may have to say?

I think this world could really be changed if everyone started giving God even five minutes a day of quiet time.

Dear God, give me the courage to be still and know you and hear the direction you would have me take. *Amen.*

November 12

Somewhere I have read that there is only one basis for really enjoying life and that is to know God. The key words here are *enjoy* and *know*—because we so seldom let ourselves go in God to really experience such fulfillment in living. We seem afraid of true joy and so put up our own roadblocks of excuses. What joy would be ours if we could only realize that life is worth living and that we have nothing to fear, either from true commitment or the quiet love of God that comes from knowing him!

We should begin each day by dedicating it to God, asking him *to accept us* as we are at this moment and *to teach us* to know him better through joyful service. This quiet moment can give us the lift that the sunrise gives each new day.

November 13

John 10:14—18

While on vacation, we drove through the Navajo Reservation. We saw the shepherds watching over their flocks and keeping them safe.

I thought to myself, *How lucky they are! They have so much solitude and are so free to be with God.* I suppose many of us long for the mountain quiet rather than the valley hustle and bustle.

Christ, too, needed solitude and often spent the night alone with God. From these times of prayer came the power to live and teach a life of love.

The solitude of the shepherd was a wonderful reminder of Christ's love for us—his sheep—and of how precious our quiet time with God should and can be.

November 14

O, God, I am grateful that you seem close to me when tragedy is all around me, when someone I love is distressed, in time of sickness, or even when I feel the most lonely. Let me feel your presence, too, in times of joy, excitement, pleasure, and contentment.

Help me, dear God, to continue to develop the art of listening, of seeking a time of quiet when my mind is not caught up in the whirl of the day's activity. Help me to hear what you say but not feel that I must find an answer to every question.

Please, God, if my only quiet time is when I iron, let me find joy in knowing you are with me then and will abide with me. Help me to think of you as my constant companion.

November 15

How do we know God? I've always felt that we can never know God fully because as we grow and mature we find new depths to our understanding of him and his desires for us.

I've often wondered why we don't think of God more often as a friend and just visit with him—talk over our day with him or just sit and enjoy his company. Usually the only time we're quiet with God is during a formal prayer time. Why not visit with him while we're ironing or doing dishes, when we really have a minute to ourselves?

What an injustice we do ourselves when we fail to recognize the presence of our greatest friend and companion, who is with us twenty-four hours a day!

Dear God, thank you for being my friend now and always.

November 16

One question that we were asked during a recent lay witness mission was, "What is your greatest need?"

Many things crossed my mind, but the thought of God came last. Why do we think of material needs and desires first? God will take care of all our problems—material and spiritual. We are told he knows what we need before we ask.

My greatest need is discipline. It takes discipline to know God—to give ourselves up totally to him all the time. We often feel that he can't be interested in the mundane aspects of our life. But if we don't cure ourselves of this attitude, we lose much time with God. Whether my life is quiet or active, I hope to satisfy my greatest need—to truly know my God—through discipline.

November 17

During a lay witness mission, we talked a lot about expecting miracles in our lives, in our church, and among each other. Something really wonderful happened, too. We saw and felt miracles taking place—people opening up to one another and becoming aware.

We often sit back and wait for our miracles. We have to help make them happen by putting our faith on the line through action and prayer and in our own lives.

That is why, to me, our prayer life seems truly important. It sets us free from ourselves and enables us to open up to people and situations. Then we see miracles happen.

Dear God, as I listen to you in my quiet times, teach me to become open to the needs of those around me.

Jackie Metcalf, Albuquerque, New Mexico

Gratitude • November 18—24

IT TAKES A LOT

November 18

Matt. 5:43—48; 16:24—26

Gratitude is fundamental to the Christian life. Its demands are too outrageous except for a person who is overwhelmingly grateful for God's love. Love our enemies? It is hard enough to love family and friends, let alone the hateful enemy. Yet God loves the just and the unjust and he expects his followers to have an all-inclusive love also. It takes a lot of gratitude.

Deny ourselves? But it is self-fulfillment that we are looking for, not self-denial. Did Jesus see that what one person feels is necessary for her own self-fulfillment may infringe upon the fulfillment of another? Self-denial and sacrifice are at the heart of the Christian life. It takes a lot of gratitude for God's love in order for one to attempt to be a Christian.

BUT IF GOD LOVES, WHY ... ? November 19
1 John 4:19—21

Even as we give thanks for God's love, we must face the question that a thoughtful child often asks, "If God loves people, why is there so much trouble—starvation, floods, wars, disease?" Jesus saw the sorrows of others and wept over them. But weeping was not all he did. He constantly ministered to human need. In his teaching he never allowed love of God to be separated from love of neighbor—love that was defined in terms of meeting the needs of others.

The Christian is often overwhelmed by the needs he sees. Yet each Christian who has experienced the love of God and is grateful for it will reach out with that love in some way. "We love, because he first loved us" (1 John 4:19, RSV).

COMPLAINING OR GRATEFUL? November 20
Phil. 4:4—13

Is complaint or gratitude the basic characteristic of our lives? What a letdown we get from the person who finds reason for complaint and bitterness in all circumstances! But what a lift, from a person who finds reason for gratitude in any situation!

Unless we are truly grateful, there is no possibility that we shall ever be satisfied. A materialist has been defined as a person who feels that he is never paid enough for what he does and always has to pay too much for whatever he gets. Jesus lived a life of gratitude—for flowers and birds, for simple daily bread, for people, and for God's love. He did not worry about whether he was paid enough.

REJOICING IN THE RIGHT

November 21
1 Cor. 13:1—6

Love "does not rejoice at wrong, but rejoices in the right" (1 Cor. 13:6, RSV). What can be more natural than not rejoicing at wrong and rejoicing in the right? Yet, if we are honest, must we not admit that occasionally we have rejoiced at some wrong that has befallen a person we felt deserved it? Who has not secretly enjoyed the wrong done by someone else because it made us look good by comparison? Are we sincerely grateful for the good that others do and the good that comes to them or does envy rear its ugly head?

A Christian who is truly grateful for God's love knows that love is sufficient for him and is freed from pettiness and envy to rejoice sincerely in the right.

GRATEFUL THAT
WE ARE NOT LIKE OTHERS?

November 22
Luke 18:9—14

We probably will not thank God that we are more virtuous than others—not with the parable of the Pharisee and the tax collector to remind us that we shouldn't. But we may witlessly thank God that we enjoy luxuries while others are naked, homeless, and starving, as though this situation were the result of divine will rather than our greed. Instead, we ought to ask forgiveness for our greediness and seek guidance in how to distribute the materials of God's earth according to his will.

It would seem that people who have perfected the hydrogen bomb and put men on the moon could find a way to feed, clothe, and house every person adequately. Can it be that we accomplish only what we really want to accomplish?

CAN WE DWELL TOGETHER?

November 23

Gen. 13:1—6

Are we grateful for people? Abraham and Lot were probably thankful for each other, but they appeared to be even more thankful for their great possessions—the possessions that made it impossible for them to dwell together. Today we are thankful for the machines and gadgets that make our lives comfortable but also pollute the land, air, and water, perhaps to such an extent that it will be impossible for us to dwell upon the earth together much longer.

Is it not greed that is causing these problems? We are greedy for more and more consumer goods. In industry the greed for profits prevents manufacturers from facing the problem of pollution responsibly. True gratitude—for God's love, for life, for people—drives out greed.

THE CHRISTLIKE LIFE

November 24

Phil. 2:1—8

Can this be the real meaning of Christian gratitude—to be so grateful for God's gift of life and for his love that we say, "This is enough; I do not need to strive for more for myself; I will devote my efforts to bringing God's love into the lives of others, with no feeling of deprivation, no martyr complex"? Is this not the Christlike life—to be more concerned with the rights of others than with one's own rights, to be unwilling to accept luxuries while others lack necessities?

This is not a way of life that we can achieve easily or sustain long. We have to work at it and hope to achieve now and then a few flashes of Christlike living. We dare not be proud of them, if we do achieve them.

Alice Massay, Grafton, Virginia

In the World but Not of the World • November 25–December 1

November 25

John 17:15–16

Picture a diver descending into the sea in a bathysphere. He is in the sea but not of the sea. He is not swallowed up and destroyed by his environment. He is free to enjoy the mysterious life forms there, to gain new knowledge and understanding, perhaps even to profit from the venture. But this freedom of movement is possible only because of the housing mechanism in which he dives. The diver is protected by a trustworthy machine.

To be in the world (as we need to be, for it is God's) and yet not of the world would be as impossible as diving to great depths without help. God has given us that help in Christ—in whom we can move freely, learning new things, enlarging the bounds of our lives.

THANKSGIVING

November 26

Psalm 24:1–2

Sometimes it helps me to look at the world through the clear eyes of a child:

Dear God, I sure do like your world. It is pretty—even when it's dark! Mamma says you made it all. That was a big job, I'll bet, even for you! I have some good friends here. There's my dog, Scooter, and two birds in the bush by the corner of the house. And my brother, too—I guess.

I like the way you do things, like make snowflakes so cold and raindrops so wet. And I like to lie on the creek bank and watch all those skittery bugs and things. *How* did you do that? I think you colored things real nice—trees and clouds and even people! God, I'm glad you gave me such a swell Mamma and Daddy. Life is sure good. But I'll bet you knew that already! Your friend, Bobby.

ON BEING ALIVE / November 27
Psalm 27:1—5

A home in my neighborhood was visited by Sorrow and the family allowed him to become a permanent member of the household. Since he came, several years ago, the curtains have never been washed, the eaves have not been painted nor the roof repaired, nor has anything been done that would lift the spirits of the occupants. When Sorrow came, friends offered help and consolation but the family chose to let life stand still. How sad, when they have a son struggling into young manhood!

Life is a precious gift. Our bodies tell us this, even when our spirits are not sure. We struggle to breathe even when we are not affirming the will to live. God has given each of us the capacity for a great zest for living. May he grant us also the ability to rise to every occasion.

ON LOVING ONE ANOTHER / November 28
Romans 12:10

In our church, we have a remarkable young adult Sunday school class. It has caught, somehow, the ability to allow everyone in the class to be a person, whether or not everyone agrees on ideals or principles. The class is unaware that it combines all the requirements for good citizenship. The members give each other freedom for self-expression. And each is free to express himself. Each person is also responsible for his thoughts and actions, weighing and measuring them verbally or silently. Each feels the same responsibility for the welfare of his fellow members.

What a rare combination! This class is a good example of what the Christian ethic really is—the interaction of freedom and responsibility in love.

TOP PRIORITY

November 29
Luke 12:27–31

My grandmother used to tell us, "Always use your best manners for the most important people—your family!" And she always added, "First things first!" A simple admonition—but one that is hard to follow. We usually save our best for visitors. Baking something special brings the question, "Who's coming?"

God is not a visitor. He's at the head of our tables, in the midst of family discussions and decisions. He goes to work with our husbands, to school and play with our children, to church with us all. First things first! Give your best to those who love you best and those whom you love best.

Give top priority to God—the love, the trust, the faith, the living of life to our Father who lives in us.

CREATED

November 30
Gen. 1

A mockingbird awakens me early each morning, singing his "Variations on a Theme." But I can't begrudge the loss of sleep to his joyful music!

This vibrant tribute of praise is synonymous with prayer.

It says, "We are of the world—God made us. We are in the world—God made it. It is beautiful! Great! Miraculous! Perfect!"

I rejoice with my singing friend, at the chance to experience it all.

All glory and majesty be thine, O God. *Amen.*

How Firm a Foundation   December 1

Matt. 7:24—27

How much fun it is to watch a group of four-year-olds sing the old song "The Wise Man Built his House upon the Rock!" They sturdily act out the efforts of a man nailing together his earthly house and show with great enthusiasm its crashing fall when it is built upon the sand of the world. Then, with the same joyful, sweeping gestures, they show the firmness of God's foundation for life.

In such a rousing demonstration, we grasp the basic truth that has been proven countless times—"The Lord is my rock, and my fortress, and my deliverer; my God, my strength . . ." (Psalm 18:2, KJV). Many times we have seen this truth in people we know—people who are involved in the world but are God's people.

Kay Stegall, Florence, Alabama

Advent Begins • December 2—8

December 2

Deut. 6:4—9

Of all the seasons throughout the church year, perhaps the one that lends itself most readily to family devotions is the season prior to Christmas, known as Advent. Of all the symbols that are used in worship at Christmastime, perhaps the Advent wreath is one of the most significant. In the home, children love to light the candles on the wreath. Everyone in the family can take part—reading the Advent scriptures, sharing in prayer, and singing for a few moments together.

O God, as we prepare our hearts for the coming of Christ, help us to appreciate our traditional ways of celebrating but also to discover new means of worshiping together. This is a fun season but it's also a holy season. Help us to remember that. *Amen.*

December 3

Isa. 40

Advent is the season of preparation, penitence, and expectancy. "Prepare ye the way of the LORD" (Isa. 40:3a. KJV), cries out the voice in the wilderness; cries out John the Baptist, the forerunner; cry out the singers in the musical, *Godspell*—"Long live God!"; cries out each one of us."

"Make straight in the desert a highway for our God. . . . A voice says, 'Cry!'

And I said, "What shall I cry?" (Isa. 40:3b, 6a, (RSV).

In the period of Advent we recognize our needs spiritually and psychologically. Advent is the readying of the believer's mind and soul, not only for the anniversary of Christ's coming as a babe but also for his present coming into the hearts of those who love. "Prepare ye the way of the LORD!"

December 4

Mark 12:41−44

What could be more exciting than the season of Advent? Christmastime conjures up for us a gallery of cheerful pictures all outlined in sharp detail from childhood memories—carols, snow, stockings, trees, toys, cards, holly, mistletoe, cookies beautifully decorated, family fun and games. A subtle something permeates the air at Christmastime that warms hearts, opens purse strings, makes tired mouths smile. But what about a family effort to spread goodwill beyond our inner circle of relatives and friends? A news report says that we in America spend $600 a year per family for toys. As a part of our preparations in the season of Advent, let us remember the words of the Lord Jesus when he said that it is more blessed to give than to receive.

December 5

Psalm 1

Blessed is the woman who walks not in the counsel of the wicked, nor stands in the way of sinners, nor sits in the seat of scoffers; but her delight is in the law of the LORD, and on this law she meditates day and night.

She is *like a tree* planted by streams of water, that yields its fruit in its season, and its leaf does not wither. In all that she does, she prospers.

She is like a tree! The evergreens symbolize God's gift of life and growth and life to come.

Why does the psalmist compare a good person to a growing tree?

Think about this rich symbolism as your family includes the Christmas tree in the celebration of Advent.

December 6

Luke 2:8–14

The covers of the December issues of two magazines in the decade of the 1970s are still vivid in my memory.

In the first year of its publication, the cover of *Catalyst* (December, 1970), a magazine for youth of the Christian Church, carried this message: "for the 1,970th time, peace, good will among men, please."

In the first year of its publication, the cover of *Ms.* (December, 1972), the women's liberation magazine, carried this message: "Peace on earth, good will to people."

Perhaps this year we could combine and contemporize them and contemplate the following message:

"for the 1,973rd time,
peace on earth, good will among people,
please!"

December 7

History has spoken often of decisive battles fought; of spears, swords, guns, bombs, and ammunition bought; of land to gain or reobtain and the many victories sought. Of the world's great war leaders, we've all been taught. But lest we think that battles are the crucial part of life, and thus continue countless efforts in any further strife, let's contemplate the other side; hold back the knife and ask about the babies born to mother and to wife. The infant Jesus, almost killed while still within his cradle, by Herod, a destructive man! What if this had been fatal? How can one calculate a loss of this much scope when the potential of a baby's life is the ground of all our hope?

Please, Lord, give us new abilities to cope with a world that's not yet seen that peace and life mean hope.

December 8

Isa. 9:2, 6—7

It is not astounding that God came down to earth. He had visited people spiritually before. He once filled a desert shrub with his presence and glory, and it burst into flames. Again, he descended upon a great mountain and, as he gave the commandments to Moses, that mountain quivered and quaked with his presence. Even before Moses, God had spoken to Abraham and provided him with a ram to sacrifice instead of his young son, Isaac. Yet the amazing thing is that in the fullness of time, "the Word became flesh and dwelt among us, full of grace and truth" (John 1:14a, RSV). As one theologian has expressed it, God became like a human being so that we might become like God.

Ginger Brittain Jarman, Fort Worth, Texas

The Meaning of the Family Today • December 9–15

ON FAMILY DYNAMICS December 9

Matt. 20:20–28

Many factors play a part in the dynamics of the family. All the people that each of us meets during a day; our inner feelings of success or failure; our secret thoughts, wishes, and needs; the tasks that each day demands we complete; the fatigue from these tasks; the order that each of us places on priorities within and beyond the family; our knowledge of all these factors in each other; our knowledge that God is out there and in here within the four walls of home—these and many more make up the dynamics of the family. A stumbling block occurs when we think only of ourselves, forgetting God and others. To know that even Jesus' Twelve stumbled, too, helps us.

Dear God, make us aware of you and others in all that we do. *Amen.*

ON PLANNING AND LIVING December 10

Luke 1:5–56

Sometimes it seems difficult to find the depth of faith that gave Mary and Elizabeth the strength to accept and rejoice in the unplanned-for, unexpected blessings that God's gift of life brought. When I read and reread this passage in Luke, I am overwhelmed by the joy of acceptance in these two women who truly knew God. How often we let our faith falter at small, everyday crises! Yet these two women were told that their whole lives were going to be changed. There was nothing either could do about it; and both rejoiced. Does our faith bring us such joy or do we become burdened down by the inevitable, unplanned-for experiences in life?

Father, grant us the faith to recognize your gifts and to rejoice in them. *Amen.*

ON LOVE AND THE UNLOVELY December 11
Luke 5:27−32; 6:37−38

Those scruffy kids with the dirty jeans and uncombed hair who congregate near the school—are *they* God's children? I see them smoking; gossip says they play around with games deadly to children twice their age—drugs, sex, petty theft, vandalism. But—they are God's children, aren't they? They arouse many emotions in me. *Fear!* They seem to threaten the innocence of my beautiful scrubbed children and their friends. *Anger!* Somebody somewhere hasn't cared enough to nurture the beauty in them. Who? Why? *Sorrow!* We live in a neighborhood of apparent affluence. Why can't we give those children something of real value—love and joy in living?

God, our Father and theirs, show me how to help them find their way. *Amen.*

ON SAYING NO December 12
Matt. 26:38−39

I'm afraid of the word *No.* I think of it as negative, final, forbidding, chastising, ugly. I wonder if I can ever overlook these obvious aspects and learn something positive about the word. As the children grow, many added dimensions and enthusiasms enter their lives. New friends have different views of life's meaning. The word *No* becomes more controversial than when family activity was the center of the children's experiences. When is the parental *No* a welcome haven from peer-group pressure? When is it an agonized cry for help from either parent or child? When is it strengthening because it affirms something strong in which we believe?

Father, help us find strength to say *No* with love as you did with your Son, our Savior. *Amen.*

ON GROWING   December 13
                              Luke 2:41–52

Our love for those in our family cannot always solve problems. Sometimes all we can do for each other is to be available if needed or to be a ready listener. Love cannot always do something but it can always be there. We don't even have to agree with those we love. We uphold certain values because we believe in them, but we can never expect our children to uphold exactly those same values. The young are of a different time with different ways. If our values are right in God's eyes, we can pray that our children will find them a worthwhile heritage; if not, with God's help and with love for each other we can try to find new values to strengthen and sustain us.

Father, give us, just as you gave to Mary, memories to keep as our children grow. Help us grow with them. *Amen.*

ON SILENCE AND WHOLENESS   December 14
                                  Matt. 9:20–22

It is as necessary to respect each other's silences in a family as it is to be ready listeners. Sometimes we need quiet and aloneness to know God and ourselves better. We need not fear to be alone with ourselves and our thoughts nor feel rejected when another needs silence and solitude. We need to be a part of each other, but we need also to be a part of God and still be wholly ourselves. Sometimes physical separation from each other is necessary in order for us to repair, alone with God, the battered selves we have become. Only God can restore us to wholeness when we have allowed life to tear us down or apart.

Dear God, give us the faith Jesus recognized when he told the suffering woman that her faith had made her well. *Amen.*

ON RESPONSIBILITY AND JOY　　　　　December 15
　　　　　　　　　　　　　　　　　　Luke 10:38−42

A sense of responsibility is important, isn't it? Each member of the family has certain jobs that are necessary and uniquely his. Sometimes, though, at the end of a long day of the tasks of motherhood, it seems that the busy work has crowded out my real responsibility—loving and nurturing one small unit of God's family. I could have taken more time to listen to the children's happy ramblings about their day's experiences. I could have listened more lovingly to my tired husband. I could have taken some time for quiet reflection and prayer. I might have been more responsible, if I had.

Father, help us keep the love and joy of Mary, without losing the responsibility of Martha. *Amen.*

Johanna Hoak, Dayton, Ohio

The Essence of My Faith • December 16−22

IF ONLY...　　　　　　　　　　　　　December 16

Not too many months ago, I was living in the "if only" realm. If only Tabetha, four, and Steven, one, were in school! You'd be surprised what miracles that was supposed to accomplish. If only we had a second car! If only I had a sewing machine!

Now, every time I start thinking "If only...," I stop and do something constructive. Peace and fulfillment come only with willingness to work where we are with what we have. Real happiness in the Lord consists not in doing what we want to do for God but in enjoying what we can do. Psychologist Carl Rogers says that we each have the ability to reorganize ourselves and our relationship to life in order to fulfill ourselves and to mature. What was that you said? *If only* you had the courage to do it?

THAT'S FOR ME!   December 17
                                  Josh. 24:14—15

In the song "What Is This?" L. S. Johnson tells about our victory in Christ in these words—joy, peace, happiness, and victory. And, boy! Is that for me!

Each of us must decide for herself what tension and goals she can live with. She must set her own values and standards and live with the consequences.

It makes no sense to me to live with discontent and anger. The only solution that offers joy, peace, happiness, and victory is the Lord.

Let's put it this way—happiness is to know an inner peace, no matter if teardrops start. The secret is Jesus in my heart.

GUARANTEED NOT TO SHRINK   December 18
                                  Eph. 2:1—10

Many of us live on the plane of self-made persons with big ideas of independence and self-reliance. We miss the guarantee and assurance of the Christian faith because we hesitate to trust only and entirely in God. In our society of seeking the easy way and the bargain, we look with suspicion on the guarantee that Jesus offered. It is really weird that we scramble for business loopholes but overlook the essence of the guarantee of our faith. Think of the sales value of faith! Here it is, friends, guaranteed to meet your present needs. Not only will it not shrink or age with use but it will grow and become better than ever. And all you want to know is how much? Well, let me tell you. Right now it is yours. You need only reach out and take it.

COULD I HELP YOU! December 19

Rom. 5:1—2

If we earned our living as salesmen for Christ, most of us would starve. We meet people with silence, apologies, or the time of the day. We hesitantly ask, "Could I help by seeing if Christ might help you?" when it is obvious that in our world Christ is the answer. We have a lifetime-guaranteed product, but most of us live as if the warranty were about to run out.

I once read an article about a new convert who just couldn't wait to attend her first church service. How glad she would be to share her joy and excitement with others who felt the same! But the service was sedate and solemn. She wondered how a faith so exciting could be celebrated with so little joy. Do you radiate joy as you proclaim, "Here's what you have been looking for!"?

PROMISES, PROMISES December 20

1 Thess. 5:12—24

I quake every time I say, "How many times have you promised not to . . ." to my four-year-old daughter. I hope God's measuring stick isn't as strict as mine. Many, many times the Old Testament recounts Israel's pledge to and departure from God. How many times I must repledge myself!

When I was eight, I decided that I would live without ever sinning. What a sense of failure I felt, not too much later, when I had to say, "Carol, you are not as good as you promised to be!" I cried and prayed for punishment and still felt only partially forgiven. "What is wrong?" I implored God. The answer came back, "Leave judgment up to me." My guilt was gone! I had been judging God's forgiveness by my standards. Unlike us, he keeps his promises—promises of full life for all who trust him.

Rejoice! December 21

Psalm 67

One of my favorite books as I was growing up was Eleanor Porter's *Pollyanna*. Pollyanna plays the "glad game." The object is to find something to be glad about in every situation. One day, when talking to the minister, with the innocence of youth she boldly asks, "Do you like being a minister?" As the conversation unravels, Pollyanna confides that her father always said he did but he also said that he wouldn't stay a minister a minute if it wasn't for the rejoicing texts—the ones that begin, "Be glad in the Lord," or "Rejoice greatly," or "Shout for joy." Did he know there were eight hundred rejoicing texts in the Bible? Pollyanna philosophizes that if God had taken all the trouble to tell us to be glad and rejoice eight hundred times, he must want us to do it—some.

Tell It Like It Is! December 22

John 3:16—21

So it comes down to us! We have the answer—a living Christ! Guaranteed not to shrink! Bringer of joy and peace and love! Full of promises of full life! Kurt Kaiser catches it for me in the song "Pass It On." He says that one spark can start a fire and soon everyone can feel its warmth. Something about God's love makes me glow. I can't contain it. I have to share it with everyone. I have to pass it on. One doesn't light a candle and then hide it under a bushel.

Tell it like it is to those you meet right where you are. Affirm to all that God sent his Son so that we might know joy, peace, happiness, and victory in him.

Carol Ann Moseley, Livonia, Michigan

Christmas • December 23–29

PAUSE FOR POWER

December 23

Psalm 23

Let God guide our busy days at this holiday season.

The Lord sets my speed, I shall not rush. He makes me stop and rest in a quiet time. He provides me with moments of stillness that restore my serenity. He leads me to be efficient and calm of mind. He gives me peace.

Even though I have a great many things to accomplish, I will not fret for I feel his presence. His power and strength keep me in balance. He gives refreshment in the midst of my activities.

By the love and grace of his Holy Spirit my joy and energy are renewed. Harmony and effectiveness are the fruits of my hours. I shall walk at the speed my Lord sets and dwell with him forever.

Let us be still and know that thou art God. *Amen.*

December 24

John 3:16–17; James 1:17

Consternation swept over me when it became my turn to deliver meals to shut-ins during the holiday week. How could I leave my family at Christmas to perform this service? But we agreed that it was a family project and we all went; the joy was ours.

The Christmas season tests our Christian stewardship, especially in terms of time and money spent for others. Lonely and needy people should claim our concern. A gift to them is a gift to him who said, ". . . as you did it to one of the least of these . . ., you did it to me" (Matt. 25:40, RSV).

Our heavenly Father, provide us with strong minds, great hearts, true faith, and ready hands so that we may serve thee always. *Amen.*

A CHRISTMAS PRAYER   December 25
                                    Matt. 6:33

Lord, grant me a growing capacity to understand and respond to the suffering of others. Fill me with a sense of duty, softened with love; a recognition of work as a privilege; a desire for justice, accompanied by mercy. Give me a task to do that has abiding value; a sense of humor; grace to forgive and the humility to be forgiven; the willingness to praise others; and the freedom to enjoy dreams. Watch over me while I take a few moments of quiet amid the noise and fret of these busy days. Let me see again the lowly shepherds on a hill and wise men hastening from afar. Let me hear again angel voices sweet and mild and feel again the presence of thy Holy Spirit. *Amen.*

December 26
Rom. 14:17–19; 15:33

Peace, joy, and happiness are almost synonymous. The dictionary suggests that a happy person is one who enjoys peace and is joyous. Happiness is also defined as a state of well-being that come from knowing God. As we celebrate "Never have so many had it so good and felt so bad about it." Abundance of material things may be having it "so good," but this cannot provide the inner peace and well-being that come from knowing God. As we celebrate the birth of Jesus, let us strive for the true happiness that only he provides through his great love. God loved the world so much that he gave his only Son so that we might have eternal life.

Be merciful unto us, O Lord, and grant us thy peace and joy as we serve thee with our lives. *Amen.*

December 27

Luke 2:20; John 14:6a

The stars and angels had disappeared and the shepherds had returned to tend their flocks. Bringing gifts, the wise men had made their visit to the newborn babe. These men of long ago experienced a fantastic spiritual happening. The promise of a Savior had been fulfilled, and never again would they be the same. They went away glorifying and praising God. Many of us, too, have had mountaintop experiences—times when the full impact of God's love seemed to encompass us. Try now, if you will, to envision that scene when the angels sang above the Judean hills; try, if you will, to count the promises fulfilled in your life. Then come away praising and glorifying God.

Lift us up, O Lord, to do thy will so that we may be worthy of thy rich promises. *Amen.*

December 28

1 Tim. 6:11–12; Eph. 6:11

At Christmas we are all wearing jewels of Christian virtues—humility, tolerance, unselfishness, kindness, goodwill and love. But by the time the tree is taken down and the decorations put away, our jewels are somewhere in a drawer ready for next Christmas. Jesus wore his jewels at all times; they were never put away. The life that began at Bethlehem offers a challenge to us to wear our jewels of Christian character all year long and seek to practice their meaning. After nearly 2,000 years, the world still knows Jesus as the most lovable of all men—the Son of God who became the Son of man so that we might all become the sons and daughters of God.

O Lord, give us a greater desire to follow thee, always wearing the jewels of the Spirit. *Amen.*

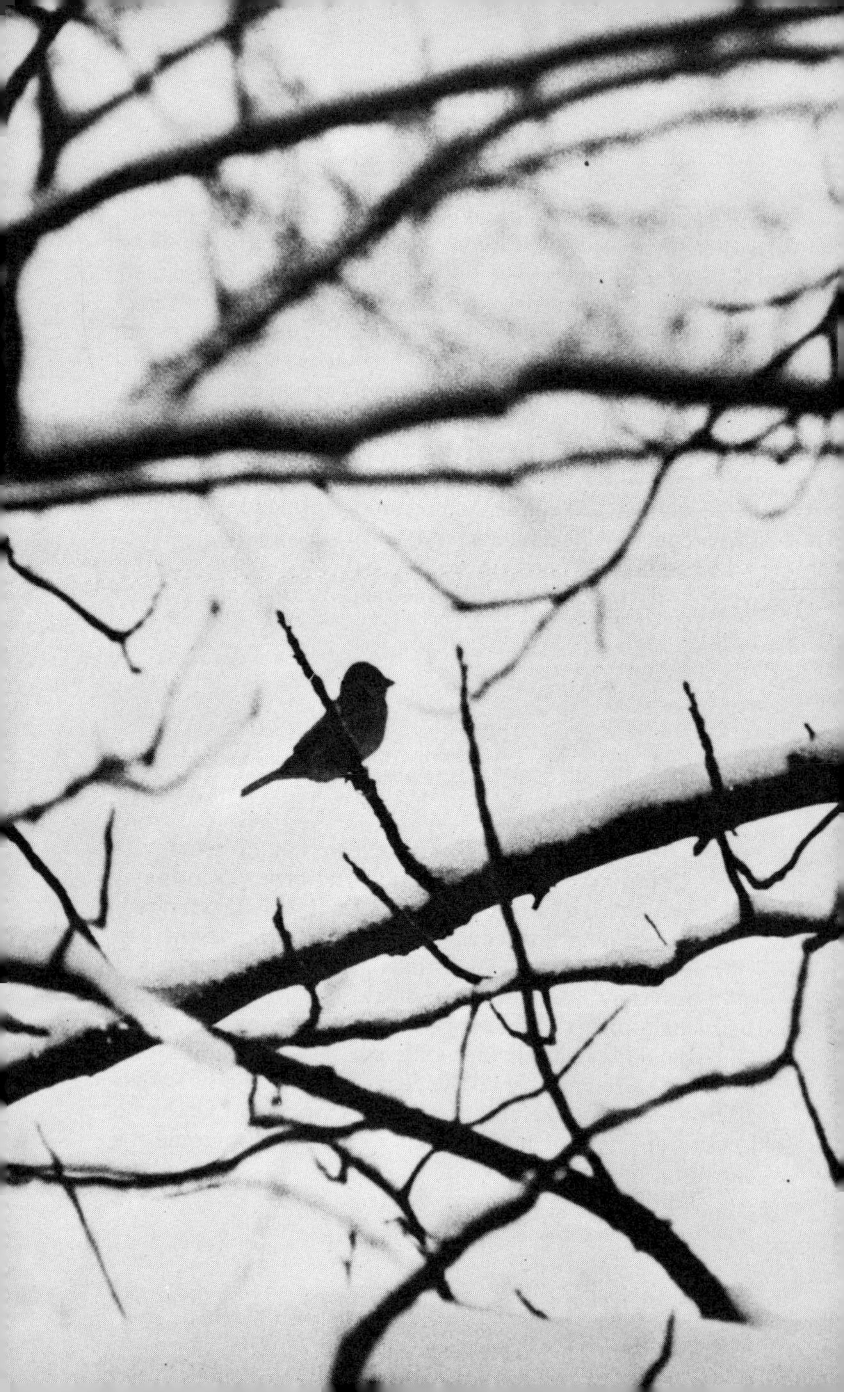

December 29
Phil. 3:12—16

Businessmen take an annual inventory of their stock and profits to evaluate their progress. This may be a good thing for Christians to do. Just ask yourself, Have any of my ideas changed lately? Have I talked recently with anyone whose outlook and way of life are quite different from mine? Did I work this year to preserve what needs preserving and to change things that need changing? Have I goals for my life? If so, do my long- and short-term goals complement each other? As we reflect on our actions of the past months, may God give us the grace to be honest with ourselves and lead us to a more positive effort in the new year that lies ahead.

All honor and glory to thee, O Lord, our God. *Amen.*

Lois Howlett, Regina, Saskatchewan, Canada

Begin • December 30—January 5

BEGIN WITH PRAYER December 30

On your mark, get set, go! A race begins with preparation. Get on your mark with prayer. Prayer is the best of all beginnings, whether for the day's living or the night's rest, a meal or a journey, a new task or an old job, new relationships or reconciliation, an offering or a sacrifice.

Get set. Pray with expectancy and get set to live expecting results from prayer. Have faith in God even if it is only the size of a mustard seed.

Go! Meet the new day, the new task, the new encounter with assurance. Greet the repeated task, the job, the life-sharing with newness. Newness and assurance are found by beginning the day with a talk with God.

God, be in all my beginnings. *Amen.*

BEGIN WHERE YOU ARE   December 31

We often make excuses for our failure to act. We say that we lack the ability to serve through community action; we aren't talented; we are short in the personality area; we have inadequate training. These reasons express the negative. Let us look, instead, at the positive.

We can speak words of comfort and encouragement to another. We can use our hands to serve another. Our money offerings help meet needs. We can volunteer to share with others whatever gift of life we have. For some unclear reason, when we think in terms of service, we often think of serving far away. Yet most of our servant actions are needed where we are. No talent is too small to use, no place too near to share it with others. Let us start where we are with what we have.

BEGIN NOW   January 1

There is no time like the present. Today will never come again. The opportunities that exist today may be gone tomorrow. Time is a gift from God. Let us make each minute count. Let us enjoy being, now.

It is easy to miss small wonders and blessings. Special events, things, and people attract our attention more easily. The everyday things and people can become commonplace. But even the routine is appreciated for the service it renders, when seen through eyes looking at the now.

Yesterday's memories we can cherish or discard. Tomorrow's possibilities we can develop or ignore. Today we are. A gift of twenty-four hours is ours to use now.

BEGIN LISTENING January 2

"Listen to me!"

That plea often jolts us back to reality. Through careless ways, we learn to pretend to listen. Sometimes listening is a difficult task. Sometimes listening is the most we can do for another. True listening demands all our attention, interest, and concern. That adds up to our all. What greater gift have we to give one another than all of ourselves? There was One who once gave all of himself for others. . . .

Listening through meditation is another form of hearing. It is relatively easy to go to God with our mouths open. Let us go to him, instead, with open ears and receptive hearts.

Listen! Listen! Listen!

BEGIN RECEIVING January 3

A gift is given with good intent. When the receiver accepts the gift with gratitude, a relationship is made stronger. Life shared with others is a gift. Each is a giver and receiver. Courtesies given and received are gifts. Compliments we bestow and receive are gifts. Understanding and love turn suggestions and complaints into offerings.

Too-busy living, however, can overlook life-sharing gifts. Compliments may be rejected as we question their sincerity. Suggestions may be refused with hurt feelings. Giving loses its significance when a giver is unable to be also a receiver. When the gift, the giver, and the receiver are all accepted by the individual persons involved, then the exchange is complete.

Begin with a
Greeting to the New Day   January 4

As night passes, leaving the essence of rest, you come to bring hope and promise to this segment of living time. You arrive gift-wrapped in colors of sunrise. You are a gift from our Creator. When used with care, goodwill, and wisdom, your hours will be well spent. The minutes will be sweetened by sharing you with others in fulfilling the purpose of God.

Come, new day, together let us explore the possibilities of living. We'll find new heights to conquer and areas of doubt to overcome. *Willingly pay the price to join the race; run with courage and win with grace. Time, you were made for me. I was made to be.*

Begin Being   January 5

Do you know Me? *Was taught in church.*
Color knowledge a continuing search.
Do you need Me? *My needs abound.*
Gather life and spread it around.
Do you hear Me? *I'm all ears.*
Eyes and hearts can also hear.
Do you love Me? *Sure I do.*
Tell the world that it is true.
Do you trust Me? *My faith is strong.*
Use once daily, all day long.
We—you and I—a unity.
Reach up and out and let us *be.*

Mertie Woolcock, Barboursville, West Virginia

Youth and the Open Door • January 6—12

HUMILITY

January 6

John 10:1—11

Some seek the way to the door of Christ and never make it. Was there someone to show them the way? Many doors are open to youth today, but finding the one to the abundant life requires stretching of the mind and soul.

The need to exercise humility is of first importance. We need to humble ourselves and rid ourselves of self-pride. Christ is our example; he "made himself nothing, assuming the nature of a slave.... Revealed in human shape, he humbled himself, and in obedience accepted even death—death on a cross" (Phil 2:7—8, NEB). To reach the heights, we need to begin where we are. There are no shortcuts, nor can we open doors ourselves. We need to prepare ourselves to enter those doors which Christ opens.

Today let us try to listen—to youth.

OBEDIENCE

January 7

Matt. 6:24—28, 33—34

Today we seek the door to obedience, vital to youth and to all other age groups. Discipline in early life is important in shaping a child's future. Too much smother love and not enough mother love can make the child too weak to face the world and its adversities.

Some are impatient to attain their desires. The joy of anticipation and planning is lost in the pursuit of instant success, instant home life, or instant knowledge.

Others, often through fear of the future, place too much emphasis on amassing material wealth instead of seeking first the kingdom of God and his righteousness.

Youth who work here and abroad to help build a better world find the true values of discipline and obedience.

Today let us try to put away anxious thoughts.

INTEGRITY   January 8
                              Job 27:1—6; Psalm 18:20

Was ever anyone so tried and tested as Job? The door of integrity is very narrow and high. To pass through we must walk tall, leaving our hang-ups, half-truths, deceits, and worldly ambitions behind us. We stand stripped before our Lord; nothing is hidden.

A girl who had stopped smoking said, "I got rid of everything—cigarettes, lighter, and ashtray." Later, when she was seen smoking again, her reply to questions was, "Yes, I had locked it all away in a chest, but I kept thinking about the key."

In order for us to walk in integrity, it is important that we be completely honest with ourselves. We need to be able to stand inspection, to come directly into the light.

Today, let us try to be honest with ourselves.

COURAGE   January 9
                              Psalm 27:1—5; Acts 21:7—14

We stand today at the door to courage. Courage gives us strength when darkness surrounds us. Sometimes discouragement and fear make spiritual cripples of us and we turn to the crutches of alcohol or drugs, of false pride, anger, or resentment. Yet, in God a source of help is ever near.

I could cite many profiles in courage—prisoners of war who spent years in captivity, wives and families who awaited their return, young and old with terminal illnesses.

I recall a brave girl stricken with polio for whom the doctors held out little hope. But she repeatedly said, "Mother, don't let your faith waver. I will get well. You must believe it." Later she recovered completely. The doctors called it a miracle, but she called it faith.

Today, let us commit ourselves to such courage.

FAITH   January 10

Heb. 11:1—6; James 2:14—18

We are committed when we enter the door of faith. Not too long ago, the words *God is dead* were often heard. But could any of us think or say this as we view God's creation, which is even yet in process?

We also hear of the "communication gap." Youth are impatient with parents; parents are disgruntled with youth. But the future church will depend largely on the experience, adaptability, and confidence of young people as they give needed leadership. Let us have faith in them.

More and more compassion, kindness, courage, and integrity are noted in youth today. A young man writing from Vietnam referred to his faith when he said, "God is very real here. Were this not so, we could not go on."

Today let us try to work in faith and trust.

SERVICE   January 11

Matt. 25:31—40

Today our door leads to service. Youth serve today—in the Peace Corps, in overseas and homeland ministries, in medicine and education. God is once again calling people to feed, clothe, and love the hungry, naked, and unloved.

I saw a youth speeding by on a motorcycle. He was dirty, and his long hair was flying in the wind. I didn't know he was rushing medicine to an ailing child. I saw a girl eating a crust of bread on the bus. I didn't know she was a stranger in a strange land, subsisting on meager funds while she learned to be a teacher. I saw a black child delivering papers in the early morning. I didn't know he was the only support of an ailing mother. Then, as I came to know you, Lord, I came to know these others who serve.

Today, let us take joy in some service we can give.

LOVE January 12

John 3:16−17; 1 Cor. 13

Joy is complete as we enter the final door—the door of love. Think of it as a giant step; here we encompass all commitments. We might ask, "What does our world need most?" Youth's answer would be *love*—the selfless giving of time, money, talents—the sharing and spreading of joy and goodwill in the spirit of Christ. It is easy to love someone we like, but what of the unlikable—the drug addict, the alcoholic, or even just that unfriendly, troublesome neighbor? We may loathe the sin but we dare not loathe the person. All of us, like the prodigal son, have the opportunity to return to the fold, gaining admittance through the door of love to abundant life.

Let us thank God for the saving grace of Jesus Christ.

Hannah B. Hubbard, Stevensville, Montana

Run to the Cry • January 13−19

January 13

Matt. 25:40

Surely God had the thought of this verse in mind when he created woman. She is sensitive to suffering and need. She listens for fretful cries of hunger, sickness, or helplessness. She sees farther than shivering in icy winds and rain to jobs and warm clothing. Her mind, busy with ways to alleviate suffering, is directed by her Creator because she is willing to serve.

The happiest woman I know is totally involved in running to the cry. Taking no time for herself, she directs friends and family in ways of helping others. No problem is too big or too small. She's poised, ready to run to the cry—sensitive, concerned, and loving. I love her!

God bless those who have ears that really hear.

January 14

Running to the cry can be the greatest adventure in Christ one can have. In our concern for others, something beautiful happens to us. God's Spirit brightens our faces. We want to laugh uproariously in the sheer joy of working with him.

Away up in the mountains of northern Idaho is Grangeville, where live some women with pretty, happy faces. A close group, they share in filling the needs of their church and community. Snow, icy roads, or fog never stop them as they answer someone's cry for help. They know they serve Christ as they venture out to help others in desperate circumstances.

Father, help us, too, to become more sensitive.

January 15

I heard something today. A woman was asked to accept responsibility in our Fellowship and she backed away, saying, "Let someone else do it. I'm busy. Besides, I have done enough!" (And this was the day I forgot my soapbox!)

A younger woman was crying for help—for some guidance as she tried to lead women in meaningful service.

Do we decide when we have done enough? Some do but, thank God, most work for him until they are through with life. There *never* comes a time we can sit back, resting on our laurels. When we do, we're dead.

O God, please forgive us when we fail. (Yes, someone else ran to the younger woman's cry. God bless her!)

January 16

There are many cries for help today. Even in the face of these cries some persons believe they have a right to withdraw from the world. Life surges downstream like the mighty Columbia River, deepening, widening, and growing greater as it passes desert or scraggy mountains on its tortuous drive to the sea. We must swim with it, not ignore it.

She sits, young of face, with dark hair, smiling as she rocks. She is friendly until I ask questions that bring her into today. Then a curtain falls over her eyes and she withdraws to her "perfect" world. Certainly life hurts. It's the hurt that hones us into beautiful creatures for God, the Father.

Run to the cry of new life in Christ, woman.

January 17

One of the finest examples of running to the cry was when The Boeing Company stopped work in Seattle in 1970 and thousands were laid off work. Everyone ran to help. Food banks were set up and manned. Salaried people bought extra for those with no paychecks. Gardens flourished all over the area and the produce kept families alive, literally.

Later Boeing got back into the stride of things again. Fortunately, needs are not always that drastic, but other emergencies arise from time to time. Some people find these tragedies stimulating and admit that they miss the urgency. They like being needed.

Thank you, Father, for turning disaster into blessing.

January 18

There is something thrilling about running to the cry—leaving ourselves open for divine direction. As an officer in CWF in our Northwest Region, I frequently responded to a cry for help in small rural communities.

One night, I was zooming alone in my car past rolling wheatfields on my way to eastern Washington. I came to a knocked'over signpost. Now which way must I take? Breathing a prayer, I felt the car pull right. Wondering, I turned right and sped on. Such blackness! I glanced at the gas gauge. Empty! Expecting the car to "fuzzle" out, I kept going. Cresting a hill, I saw my destination below, spread all over the valley—thousands of twinkling lights. I think you know the car ran on something besides gas.

Thank you, Lord.

January 19

As God's children, we can do anything, God willing! If we're challenged to run to the cry, dare we say, "I can't" or "I don't want to"—turning our backs on those who need help? I was taught as a child that this little game could be played two ways. Our heavenly Father might say, "I won't" or "I can't right now." Wouldn't that be awful? When we need him, we need him right now.

Running to the cry keeps us alert, bright-eyed, full of joy because we're needed, fulfilled by accomplishment, appreciative for small blessings, and *excited.*

Lord, thank you for such a rich, full life. As we do it for the least of these, we do it for you.

Ivy Fulton, Longview, Washington

Spiritual Succotash • January 20−26

PRAISE THE LORD! January 20

Isa. 61:3, 10−11

Have you ever stood naked before God—your rags of righteousness encircling your feet? I have—and the shame and embarrassment I felt was a stark lesson I'll cherish through life. Had I never been confronted with God's glorious majesty, holiness, and righteousness, I would still be mired down in my own misguided efforts to salvage my salvation. God took my filthy rags and clothed me with humility until that future day when I shall be clothed with immortality. Praise God for breaking through my consciousness to reveal the standard of excellence found only in Jesus Christ! Praise the Lord for victory through the power of the indwelling Holy Spirit! Be clothed also with the "garment of praise instead of a heavy, burdened and failing spirit" (Isa. 61:3a, Amplified Bible).

FEAST OR FAMINE January 21

2 Tim. 3:16−17; 4:1−2

Imagine sitting down to a banquet table loaded with delicious foods but, instead of eating, spending the hour discussing the utensils and the correctness of the table service. Foolish thought! Yet how often this happens in our church classes and worship services. Christians gather for a brief period to get spiritual guidance and strength for their lives. The time is consumed with meaningless questions or high-sounding philosophies that have no root in truth. They are interesting to ponder, but the spirit is not fed nor does the soul magnify God.

May God grant that we put a premium on this time that is meant for our learning and growth. May we guard against focusing attention on meaningless utensils, while a banquet of spiritual meat sits completely untouched.

THE ANVIL OF GOD'S WORD

January 22
Eph. 6:13-20

How awkward and cumbersome that thimble was! Yet I could not take it off. My teacher would insist I put it on again. Thus I learned to sew with a thimble that is now a shield to my finger and a tool I cannot do without.

In the Christian's armor is the shield of faith. Our faith reinforces and protects us from Satanic attack. Without faith we are also without hope. How do we obtain this shield? It is fashioned on the anvil of God's Word with the hammer of study. Many people fall defeated on the battlefield of life because they are not willing to persevere through a training period when their Bible is awkward to learn, handle, and understand.

"Faith cometh by hearing, and hearing by the word of God" (Rom. 10:17, KJV).

SEND US SHEPHERDS

January 23
Ezek. 34

One day, as I prayed in the Spirit, the Lord gave me a vision. I saw sheep sheared close to the skin. Each was so weak that its ribs could be counted. They were unsteady on their feet and leaned against one another for support. A chilling wind blew, and I felt desperate for their lives.

I had been struggling with the reason for the biblical ignorance and the spiritual malnutrition I had encountered in professed Christians of many years. Where are the shepherds? Why haven't the flocks been led to green pastures and beside still waters?

O, Lord, you alone are the Good Shepherd. Spare these innocent lambs and restore the flesh of your sheep. Send us more true shepherds who will lead your flock to your bountiful table where the Bread of Life is spread.

X MARKS THE SPOT January 24
Isa. 1:10−20

I watched a TV commercial take the X out of Axion and apply it to the laundry stains. Magically the soil and stain disappeared. Our clothes do become soiled, but a more urgent concern is the stubbornly soiled and stained life. I remember the first time Christ was applied to my life. I came through the process white as snow because he removed (forgave) my stain (sin). Not only does Christ remove the unbecoming areas of our lives but he also seems to have a built-in "Scotchgard" process. We do not soil as easily as before. "X marks the spot" is a slogan I endorse, if that X stands for Christ.

"And now why tarriest thou? arise, and be baptized, and wash away thy sins, calling on the name of the Lord" (Acts 22:16, KJV).

A FISH STORY January 25
John 6:47−51

A few years ago, we became tropical fish fanciers. We began with one tank and soon expanded to six. With advice from another local hobbyist, my husband set up proper conditions for various species to spawn and had gratifying success. As the fry grew, I discovered in them a parallel to a spiritual truth. Fry fed on dry food grew very slowly. Fry fed on living food (brine shrimp that we raised for the purpose) grew rapidly.

In the same way children of God who feast regularly on the living Christ show obvious progress in their growth. Those with no hunger for the milk and meat of the Word fail to mature.

Lord, let us not be satisfied until we hunger and thirst after righteousness that we may grow in grace and in the knowledge of our Lord and Savior, Jesus Christ.

ARE YOU EQUIPPED? January 26

Heb. 4:12; Acts 1:7−8

In the military a recruit is issued a rifle. His training requires that he become so familiar with it he can take it apart and put it back together blindfolded. His life depends on his knowledge and use of his weapon.

In our induction as Christian soldiers, we, too, are issued a weapon. It is the sword of the Spirit, which is the Word of God. As the rifle is useless without ammunition, so, too, is our sword useless without the power of the Holy Spirit. We are not at war with flesh and blood but with Satanic forces that work without and within. Jesus parried Satan's temptations blow for blow with the Word of God. Why don't we spend more time in prayer and study—preparing ourselves for the battles of life?

Joyce Barnes, Houstonia, Missouri

God Is! • January 27−February 2

GOD IS January 27

FOR I AM Gen. 5:1b−2a

A band of gypsies camped on our farm. I was four years old. A gypsy woman in flowing robes came to our door to ask my mother for a cup of sugar. Her long black hair, tied here and there with little red ribbons that held tiny silver bells, fascinated me as I stood beside her outside the screen door.

My mother quickly opened the door, pulled me in beside her, reached up and latched the door. The gypsy woman pointed upward. I can see that finger pointing yet! "I will not hurt your little girl. I believe in ─────── !" I do not recall the word she said for the Creator but at that moment I became aware that I am and God is!

Thank you, God, for the life you gave me. Help me to be aware of my oneness with you. *Amen.*

GOD IS   January 28
REVEALED IN NATURE'S BEAUTY   Psalm 104:13

Our workshop on Japan ended with an assignment to write some haiku poetry to share with the group the next day.

Rain had ceased; the clouds were moving eastward over the Book Cliffs near Grand Junction, Colorado. The setting sun glowed in the west, reflecting red-gold on the bare, gray cliffs and gray-blue clouds. Tears of joy came to my eyes in response to the glory of the scene. God was there! I could not help but frame my haiku thus:

> Sunset-tinted cliffs,
> A backdrop of gray-blue clouds—
> And smiles tear-sparkled.

My Father, help me always to find you in the unexpected beauties of your creation and respond to these blessings with joy and thanksgiving. *Amen.*

GOD IS   January 29
FELT IN THE WARMTH OF MARRIED LOVE   Eph. 5:33

Alone, in love and married! My husband said, "We must remember there are three of us." "Three?" I questioned. He drew a triangle on a bit of paper and wrote our names at the base corners. At the apex, he wrote "God." I understood.

Some things were "for us"—a common faith in God and a dedication to Christian service. Our different temperaments complemented each other in our marriage and work relationships. But we had human weaknesses so we made a pledge. We would not go to sleep angry with each other. You can't, kneeling in prayer with arms about the one you love and knowing that God is!

Dear God, help me feel your presence in every human relationship to strengthen and bless the ties that bind us. *Amen.*

GOD IS   January 30
SEEN IN LITTLE CHILDREN   Mark 9:37

When my daughter-in-law had a miscarriage and was to stay in the hospital overnight, I knew my four grandchildren would ask why. I asked Janet if I might tell them. "Yes, I wish you would," she replied.

That evening I gathered them about me and told them the story. All four pairs of eyes were wide with awe and compassion. Ten-year-old Laura voiced their feelings quickly. "Grandma, *why* didn't she tell us? We could have helped her more!" I saw God then. The affirmation came through sweet and clear—God is!

Father, help me see you in little children, finding there the simple trust and compassion I need to give to my neighbor. *Amen.*

GOD IS   January 31
A COMPANION IN TIME OF TROUBLE   Psalm 88:1−2

What do you do when in anguish you watch a little brother and two sisters die? When a mother is distraught and ill so you must take over the household?

Who is really near when you watch a young husband die? A son in his young manhood?

Who is near when in a hospital you help men and women "cross over" one by one?

Who is with you and a young man as you pray with him for his critically ill wife?

Who stands by you in strength and wisdom to help you cope with a mentally unbalanced young girl?

Who is light in the night of uncertainty of friendships—and even of yourself? God is!

My God, you are a very present help in time of trouble. *Amen.*

GOD IS LOVE   February 1

"This is how God showed his love for us: he sent his only Son into the world that we might have life through him. . . . Dear friends, if this is how God loved us, then we should love one another. No one has ever seen God; if we love one another, God lives in us and his love is made perfect in us" (1 John 4:9, 11−12, TEV).

Because God is love, I remember that his ways and secrets are my discovery—not my creation.

Because God is love, I am called to respond with the kind of compassion that Jesus had for the woman taken in adultery.

Because God is love, I am called to love my neighbor as myself.

Dear God, may I so love all persons in words and acts that they may know that God lives! *Amen.*

GOD IS! REJOICE!   February 2

Psalm 66:1−2

Dear God, out of the past your name has been glorified by those who searched for you through dim centuries. For those prophets, priests, and kings, I thank you.

I praise you for your wonderful gift to me—your Son, Jesus, whose life and teachings, death and resurrection revealed your love for me.

I rejoice in my heritage of men and women who knew you and were faithful to the message of reconciliation.

I rejoice that in Christ I can live victoriously, tackling with zeal and joy the problems of today, as did Caroline Neville Pearre and the women of her time.

"May your way be known upon earth—your saving health among all nations" (Psalm 67:2, KJV). *Amen.*

Ethel Darling, Denver, Colorado

Peace • February 3-9

THE NEED FOR PEACE February 3

"Acquaint now thyself with him, and be at peace; thereby good shall come unto thee" (Job 22:21, KJV).

Ever since human beings have been on this earth, they have felt the need of being at peace with themselves, with God, and also with one another. In our day, even though much has been done to obtain peace, it remains a high ideal that has not yet been reached.

In every nation, the dove is known as a symbol for peace. In some nations, the eagle, the lion, and the snake are seen as symbols of war and its destructive power.

Peace is of so high a value that every generation must transmit to the next the desire to achieve it. But only with the Lord's help will we be able to reach the peace for which the world longs.

PEACE AMID TRIALS February 4

"I was not in safety, neither had I rest, neither was I quiet; yet trouble came" (Job 3:26, KJV).

When persons find themselves in conflict or trials of any kind, they suffer great tribulation. Job, almost on the border of desperation, said that he had had no peace, as he bewailed the loss of his daughters and sons, his health, and all his possessions, and the tribulation he felt in his own spirit. This is a natural human reaction but we, as Christians who have heard and believed the message of Christ, should react to trials as children of light—as persons who have the support of Christ's promises. To be able to feel and to hold onto that personal peace, we must trust in the One who said, "Ask, and it shall be given you; seek, and ye shall find . . ." (Matt. 7:7a, KJV).

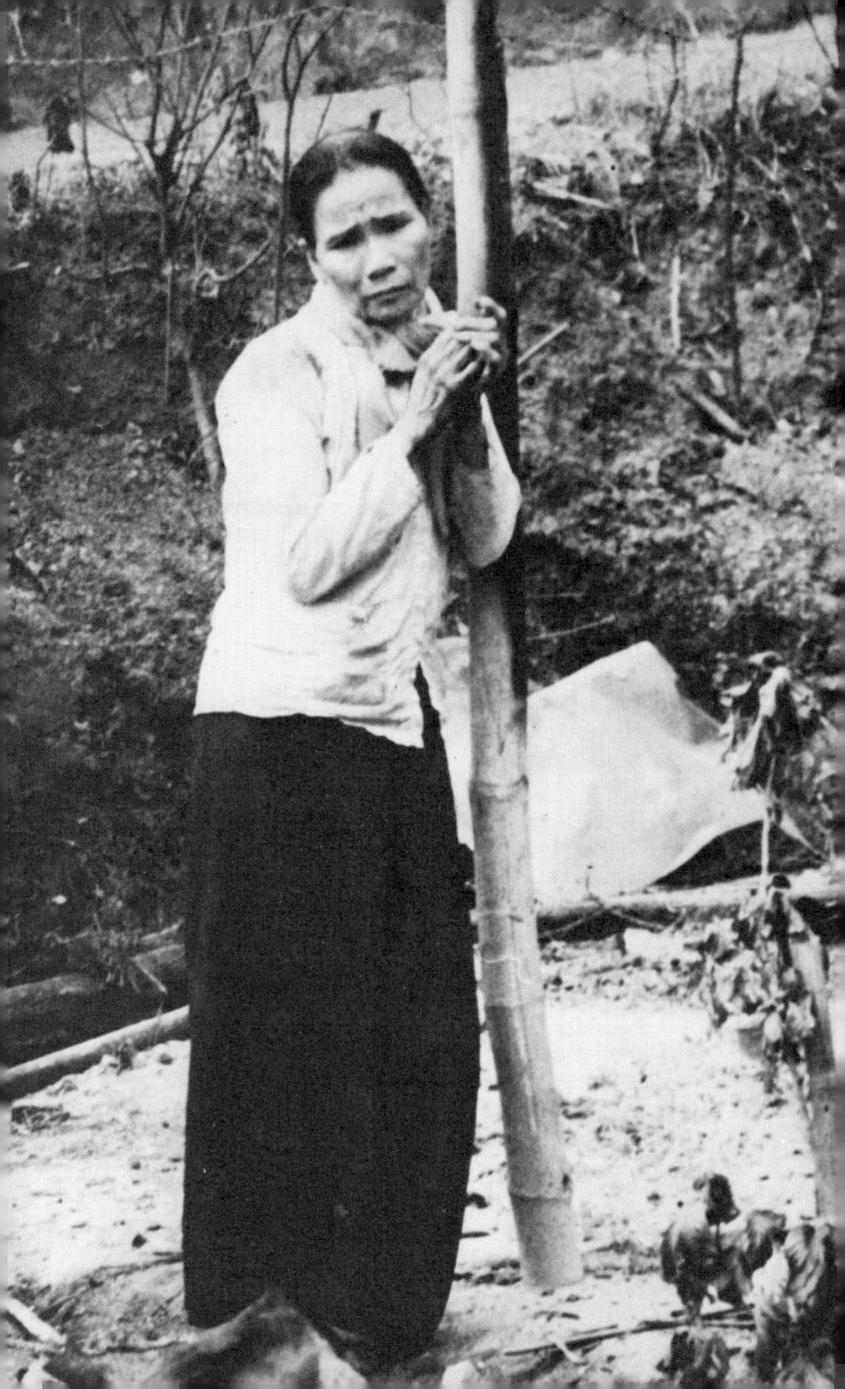

INNER PEACE																										February 5

". . . forget not my law; but let thine heart keep my commandments; for length of days, and long life, and peace, shall they add to thee" (Prov. 3:1–2, KJV).

Inner peace depends upon the communion that we can establish with the Lord and on our positive attitudes toward the trials of life. To be able to reap peace, we must sow peace within ourselves.

The seed of peace is to keep and practice the Word of God. The result of such obedience, we are told, will be an inner peace.

One of the greatest purposes of our communion with God should be to find and keep that peace in our hearts. Such peace is indispensable in establishing relations of peace with our fellow men and women.

A WORLD WITHOUT PEACE																			February 6

Almost thirty years have passed since the end of World War II, when millions of persons died. Many lives were sacrificed and much material property was destroyed in the hope that at the end we would have peace. Yet peace has not been found, though peace treaties were signed. New hostilities arose in Korea, in Vietnam, in the Middle East, in Africa. At the birth of Christ, the angels sang of peace on earth. This song is still sung and repeated efforts are being made to obtain peace, through new peace treaties, and world peace organizations, by means of social justice, and by preaching the gospel.

Let us pray that with the Lord's help we may reach that peace so desired. A world without peace is a world in bankuptcy.

AT PEACE WITH ALL PEOPLE
February 7

"If it be possible, as much as lieth in you, live peaceably with all men" (Rom. 12:18, KJV).

At times we are rebellious in spirit because, even though Christian doctrines have been taught for so many centuries, we have not yet learned to live as Christians. The proof is that people are still at war. Misunderstandings and hate exist between small nations and great nations. The voice of the Apostle Paul still speaks to us and tells us to be at peace with all people.

We know that wars are cruel and destructive. War is a wrong we should do away with, so that we may all live in peace. The Prince of Peace should live in our hearts and in the hearts of those who rule the world, so that all our efforts to gain peace will not be in vain.

PEACE WITH OUR NEIGHBORS
February 8

"Blessed are the peacemakers: for they shall be called the children of God" (Matt. 5:9, KJV).

To be peacemakers we truly need to be at peace with ourselves and with our Lord. We need to have a genuine spirit of peace toward those around us. If we live in peace, we must share it with our neighbors, our co-workers, our classmates, and all whom we meet.

Several years ago, when entering a new auditorium, I met a large group of persons who were leaving after attending a convention of automobile salesmen. To my surprise, these persons were getting into cars of different models than those of the companies they represented.

In seeking peace we, as Christians, must be sincere, living in the peace we preach.

PEACE, A GIFT FROM GOD   February 9

"Peace I leave with you, my peace I give unto you: not as the world giveth, give I unto you" (John 14:27a, KJV).

My conviction is that God uses us so that his will can be done among us. He offers us his peace because he knows that the world offers a peace that is not secure. The Lord offers to give us a permanent peace that shines in our lives and in all our acts.

To have this peace implies a responsibility toward others. We need to witness, to pray, and to work for more Christian homes; more churches where the gospel is preached; more hospitals, schools, and community centers where good citizens of the kingdom of God manifest peace and love for people.

Joyce Velazquez, Wichita Falls, Texas

The Christian Faith • February 10—16

February 10

Mark 9:14—24

The technological world of today takes pride in the instantaneous process—instant replay, instant food, instant worldwide communication. We are conditioned to believe that what we need can be obtained instantly. But faith is not an instantaneous acquisition. It comes through a process of growth, evolving out of many experiences.

The metamorphosis of a locust illustrates the struggle of changing from the old to the new. During this slow process, the embryo is a soft, pliable mass, vulnerable to outside forces. Gradually, through sheer exertion and movement, the body forms and the wings and legs appear.

Faith, too, comes through wrestling with doubts, exercising new ideas, and searching for the meaning of life. Apart from struggle, there is no growth.

February 11

Luke 10:38—42

Someone has said that an unexplored faith cannot be lived; it can only be pretended. To develop a faith takes more than listening to a sermon or a Bible lecture. It takes searching, listening, questioning, and, finally, a willingness to build a theology related to the daily experiences of life—the hurts, the joys, the anxieties, and the successes. Our lives, for the most part, are lived out in ordinary places—homes, places of employment, recreational areas, even an hour a week in the grocery store.

As we meet the demands and pressures of each day, the content, quality, and depth of our faith will determine how we respond. Jesus counsels women not to be worried and troubled over many things but to seek that which brings a higher quality of life.

February 12

Acts 3:1—10

A college student said, "I have no hope for the church. It isn't doing anything that can't be done by someone else." My first reaction was one of defense. The church has been a change agent in society, working for justice, human rights, education, and the freedom of the individual. Her evaluation was being made of the church visible to her in her experience—that is, my witness and that of the local congregation. How had I failed to witness to the fact that my faith had been the source and sustaining power compelling me to move out to be involved in the problems and life situations of my community? The church, while offering gifts of helping, healing, and reconciling, must also give evidence of a radiant, living faith that can make a difference in the lives of people.

February 13

Acts 4:1—20

As a member of the fraternal visitors' team of the Christian Church to Asia in October, 1972, I can never forget the sincerity and dedication of Asian Christians. Their deep commitment radiates as a way of life, showing that their faith is not a belief inherited from their ancestors but one that is experienced personally.

A young friend and newly baptized believer made a decision not to marry anyone who did not share her faith, though only 1 percent of the people in her country are Christian. Her choice is limited but her commitment firm.

Asked about the future of Christianity in Japan, a former Buddhist monk answered, "When one has had the experience of living in a Christian fellowship and when the spirit of Christ is a part of life, one cannot shift back."

February 14

Luke 22:54—62

Peter had been one of Jesus' closest companions, yet, under the pressure of criticism, social stress, and ridicule, he denied knowing Jesus.

A young Thai Christian asked a group of us who were visiting in Bangkok to pray for him so that he might have the strength to remain a Christian. While he was studying in the United States, he had accepted Jesus Christ as his Savior. Now he had returned to Thailand, where his friends and family, all Buddhists, knew nothing of his newfound faith. He needed the prayers, concern, and love of fellow Christians to give him courage to break the news to his family and to continue to grow in and witness to his Christian faith.

Pray that he and others like him may remain steadfast.

February 15

Luke 7:36—50

Is it a sin to treat oneself as one who has no gift? Sometimes we place an unrealistic limitation on our abilities. If we were to treat others in this way, people would say we were inhumane.

When we come to know Jesus Christ, we discover a power that takes us beyond this introspective feeling of insignificance and unworthiness to a knowledge of the power and potentiality within us. His love nourishes an inward appreciation of self and enables us to use our gifts to fulfill God's purpose in our lives.

The woman in the above scripture felt she was a nobody. Jesus recognized her as what she could become. He released the possibility of new life when he said, "Your faith has saved you; go in peace" (Luke 7:50b, RSV).

February 16

Rom. 8:18—25

"The whole creation is on tiptoe to see the wonderful sight of the sons of God coming into their own" (Rom. 8:18b, Phillips).

God must have rejoiced when the early leaders of the women's missionary movement acted upon a conviction and changed the whole concept of women's role in the church.

The Christian faith has given Japanese women freedom to contribute equally in leadership positions according to their abilities and gifts, even in a male-dominated society.

The real triumph of our faith can come in a willingness to submit to the freeing force that challenges us to discover and use our special gifts in order to move out in new areas of witness and to become what God intended us to be.

Fran Craddock, Centralia, Illinois

Listening • February 17−23

February 17

"Make a joyful noise to the LORD, all the lands! Serve the LORD with gladness!" (Psalm 100:1−2a, RSV).

When I got into my car, I heard the starter turn over as soon as I turned the key. The battery started the old car even on this cold day. While driving to the shopping center, I listened to music on the radio. I passed a school playground and heard the laughter of running and jumping children.

Sometimes we fail to notice and appreciate the commonplace things in our lives. I have a car and it works. I enjoy music, news, and drama on the radio and television. It makes me happy to hear laughing children. Joyous sounds surround me and beckon me to listen.

Lord, help me see and hear your goodness and glory in the everyday, ordinary things of life.

February 18

"He who has ears to hear, let him hear" (Matt. 11:15, RSV).

I saw an acquaintance at the grocery store. She had lost weight and looked good, and I told her so. Her face was sad as she responded, "Oh, I've been so depressed lately that I've started eating again. I've gained back five pounds!" I repeated my initial comment and we each pushed our carts down separate aisles of the store.

As I walked past the produce, I thought to myself, "Was that a cry for help? Did I ignore her request to be heard?" I needed to get home to start dinner; maybe that is why I thought only of the clock ticking away and the ring of the cash register calling me to the quick check line. People send out signals for help at the grocery store, in the exercise class, at the dinner party, and the breakfast table. Are we listening for the signals?

February 19

"Be ye doers of the word, and not hearers only . . ." (James 1:22, RSV).

Barry's twelfth birthday party was filled with laughter, games, and gifts. The children were a joy. I was serving ice cream and cake when I noticed Barry feeding Jeff. God spoke and I heard. Let me explain.

Jeff is physically handicapped. He doesn't speak clearly, can't open the door or take his coat off. When I learned that Jeff was to be at the party, I was a little apprehensive about the roughhouse that is inevitable with twelve-year-old boys.

But the boys were great! They knew Jeff and they helped him play the games he could. Fourteen sixth-grade boys enabled me to hear the voice and see the action of God's love as they recognized and responded to the uniqueness of each person present.

February 20

"He who has an ear, let him hear what the Spirit says to the churches" (Rev. 2:7, RSV).

Today I went to church. I don't mean I just went into the building. I went to *church!*

I left home expectantly. I greeted friends entering the church building and we talked and laughed together. The associate minister led us in prayer and helped to prepare us for Communion. Communion was a creative feeling and thinking time for me. I felt God's presence. I needed help; I received help.

I listened to the minister as he delivered a sensitive sermon and, after the service, I shared with him my thoughts about his thoughts. We understand and appreciate each other. The worship service helped prepare me for the week's tasks, but above all it prepared me to *be me* in all my activities.

February 21

"They have ears, but they hear not" (Psalm 135:17a, RSV).

Mary's children dashed in from school as Mary was watching her favorite soap opera on TV.

"Mamma, Mamma, guess what happened?"

"Shhh—quiet," she commanded. During the commercial she pointed out cake and milk for their snack. She tried to listen with two ears—one for her television family and one for her children. When the program closed, she noticed her son's school papers on the table. The spelling grade was lower than usual. She called to him, but he had gone out to play. Then she remembered that today was field day and Jack had been excited about competing. She wondered how he had come out in his event. But her ears had been tuned in to a TV family rather than to her own. When her children needed to share with her, she heard them not.

February 22

"A time to keep silence, and a time to speak" (Eccl. 3:7b, RSV).

I was in my exercise class. We were sitting on our mats doing arm isometrics when a small voice said, "Hi, Mommy!" It came from the nursery behind us where the baby-sitter was keeping the children.

The child's mother was facing the other way. In a quiet, mumbling voice, with her head down, she whispered, "I hear you." But the child was not satisfied with her answer.

I had a mental flashback to childhood. "Look at me when I'm talking to you," my mother was saying.

We want people to listen to us and we want to know they hear us. Giving people our attention reinforces their feelings about their own self-worth. With our eyes, face, body, and voice we need to say, "You are worth listening to."

71

February 23

"I love the LORD, because he has heard my voice . . ."
(Psalm 116:1, RSV).

My sons have a playmate who is mute. He came to our door one day and gestured to me. When he raised his hand to his shoulder, I knew he wanted Philip. I said, "Philip's out on his bicycle," and gestured as though I was riding a bicycle. He then put his hand a little higher, asking for my older son. I repeated the same bicycle action. We both smiled and waved good-bye.

We had "talked and listened" to each other. He let me know he wanted to see my sons. I let him know I was glad to see him. It is important to listen to people's words and feelings. And it is satisfying to know that God listens to ours.

Catherine Broadus, Lexington, Kentucky

Lent Begins • February 24–March 2

TROUBLES   February 24

We are tempted to feel that the best achievements of people occur under favorable conditions, when they can sing, "Oh, what a beautiful morning; everything's going my way." It's not true. History proves it.

Things were not going well for the great composer Handel. His health and his fortune were gone. His creditors were threatening him with jail. From the depths of his despair, he wrote the "Hallelujah Chorus."

Jesus, the unordained, itinerant healer and preacher, was arrested, tried (after a fashion), beaten, and crucified. On the third day, he arose and made eternal life available for all who want it enough to follow him.

God help us to use our little and our big troubles to come up with something good. *Amen.*

HUBBUB
February 25

How is my life hubbubed? Let me count the ways.

I can't get the whole house in order at the same time. If the kitchen is clean, the bedroom is in a heap. If the living room is presentable, rainboots, newspapers, and "things" clutter the hall.

I accept too many obligations. I am on too many committees. I offer and overextend myself in my children's school, in the church, in charitable drives, even in looking after my in-laws. I am a joiner; I need to be a resigner. I am too busy; I need to be still. My mind is jumpy; it longs for tranquillity

Soothe my hubbubed life, O God, before I join the ranks of the unfit—unfit to live with myself and unfit to live with others. *Amen.*

STUFF
February 26

After Saul had been chosen king of Israel, his subjects looked for him, but he could not be found. After long searching, they discovered he had hidden himself "among the stuff" (1 Sam. 10:22b, KJV).

This is the story of all too many of us. We involve ourselves in the mundane, the trivial, the unimportant and are lost to the vital purposes of life. Yes, we go astray in stocks and bonds, careers, finance, and even religion. We have no time for God's realities because we are forever buried "among the stuff."

God, give us the common sense to push the stuff aside and keep company with you every day. *Amen.*

ASH WEDNESDAY   February 27

The Lenten season begins today. This means we have six weeks to prepare ourselves for Easter and we need every moment of them. We could fill the forty days with apologies, explanations, and justifications for our present state of spiritual health. Instead, let us affirm our intentions.

We shall be carriers of love, understanding, and hope to all—even to those we have chosen to avoid in the past.

We shall abandon our tempers, our complaints, and our distrust, instead of skillfully veiling them with pretense.

We shall refuse to let the rat race and social superficialities rob life of its intrinsic values.

These are common sins, O God. We need your uncommon strength to overcome them. Help us. *Amen.*

NARROWNESS   February 28

Father, I am not sure whether I want to make a confession or just talk things out with you.

I thought I had a strong will; now I am beginning to wonder if I am immovably stubborn.

I have some principles about which I have boasted; now I realize I may have prejudice and principle confused.

I find myself condemning that which I do not understand. But couldn't understanding contribute more to relationship than agreement? Of course there is more than one way to believe, to do, and to act.

Help me out of my narrowness, O God. *Amen.*

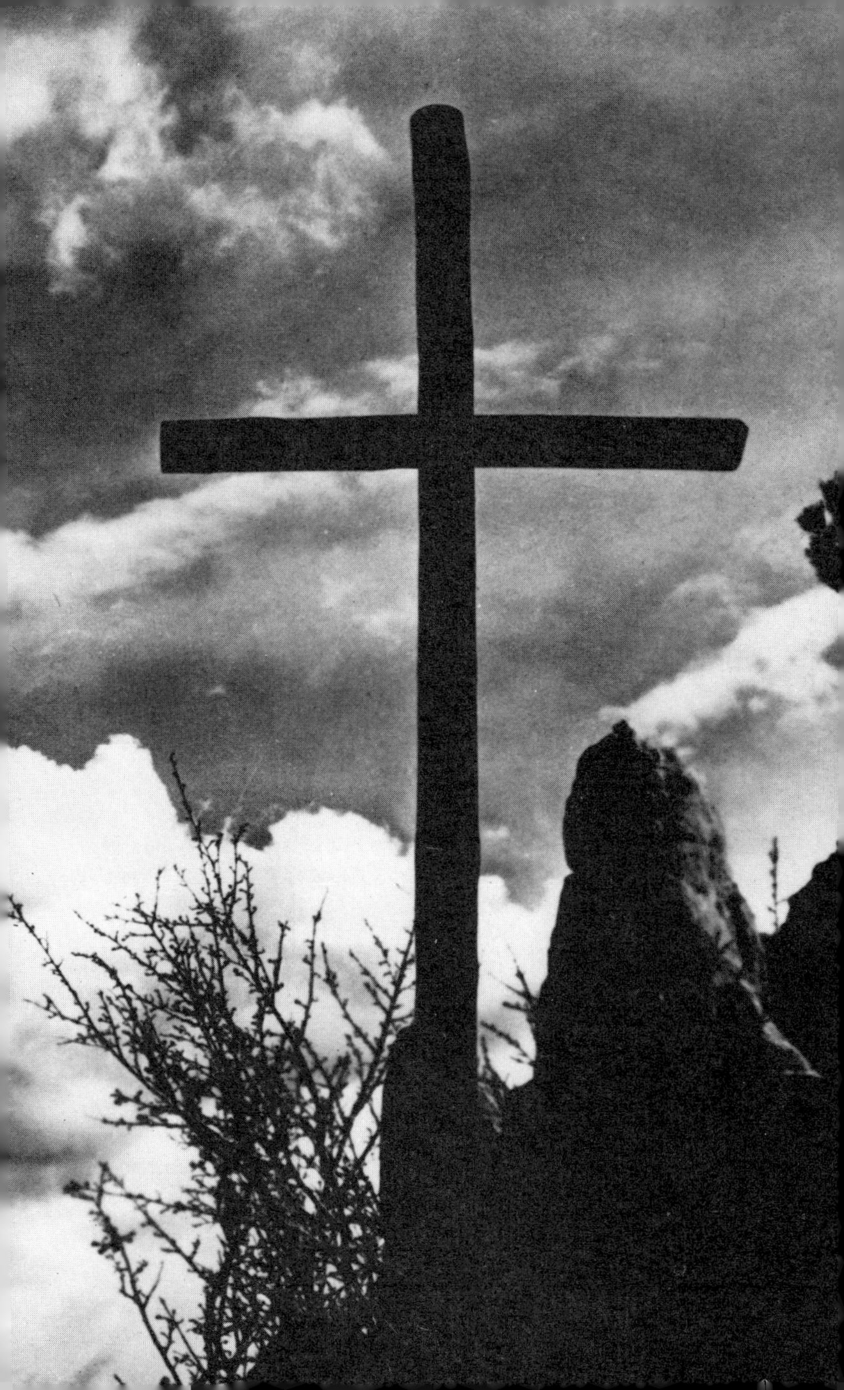

Eyes   March 1

A person's eyes reflect the soul.

Sometimes we are afraid to really look. Our shifting, cunning glances would rather not rest on people who are poorer than we, not so cultured, not so well educated, housed, fed, and cared for. Yet, we know we have no right to close our eyes nor to be selective in what we see.

We see others more often than we see ourselves. We rarely, if ever, see ourselves as we are.

We read, "The Lord turned around and looked straight at Peter" (Luke 22:61a, TEV). We also feel like going outside and weeping bitterly as Peter did.

Father, restore our vision with your Spirit because we need it. *Amen.*

Cross   March 2

Tomorrow is the first Sunday in Lent. Like my Master, I see the shadow of the Cross. Unlike my Master, I want to shirk its humiliation, its agony. He saw beyond the present. I do not. In the midst of his heartbreak, he forgave. In the midst of his suffering, he healed. I can't bring myself to do either. I am not sure I want to forgive and heal wounds.

His Cross was fashioned by people who despised him. My cross is made of timber from a tree grown in my own back yard and fashioned with my own hands. Help me stretch myself upon it, as he did. In my suffering, may I learn a truth deeper than joy can know. I need to experience an Easter morning in my life. Help me. *Amen.*

Kathleen Bailey Austin, Indianapolis, Indiana

The Miracle of Healing • March 3-9

SALVATION IN EXTREMITY
March 3
Psalm 130:1

At some time or other, all of us are faced by an overwhelming event. We stand at that moment stripped of the ordinary resources that have made our days bearably happy. The bodily comforts and ease of mind that we have known before are gone and we are gripped by agony and despair.

The words of the psalmist leap to our thoughts: "My God, my God, why hast thou forsaken me?/Why art thou so far from helping me . . .?/I am poured out like water . . . ; /my heart is like wax,/it is melted within my breast" (Psalm 22:1, 14, RSV). "My throat is as dry as dust,/and my tongue sticks to the roof of my mouth" (Psalm 22:15a, TEV).

We struggle to pray and our prayer becomes a cry for help: "Don't stay away from me, Lord!/Hurry and help me, my Savior!" (Psalm 22:19, TEV).

A LIGHT SHINES IN THE DARKNESS
March 4
Isa. 59:10a

The shock of knowing that our life's direction has been altered—that plans for days or weeks ahead must be changed and a new, painful adjustment made—causes us to suffer loss of faith and weakening of the power to live. There follows a painful groping for stability, for self-control, as the forces that led to the event are brought under conscious scrutiny—whether it was an accident on the highway, the shock of surgery that reveals cancer, the sudden malfunction of the heart. The fact that this has happened to us or to those we love makes us realize that deep aloneness often is a factor to be dealt with.

"I am weak and helpless;/come quickly to me, God./You are my helper and Savior—/do not delay, Lord!" (Psalm 70:5, TEV) *Amen.*

Take No Thought for Yesterday

March 5
Psalm 38:8

In the struggle to regain our perspective, we are often hampered by regrets. "If only I had listened.... If I had not gone.... If only I had it to do over again!" Like a child seeking a lost parent, we struggle to regain yesterday when things were beautiful and serene.

We feel imprisoned by our fate and dwell upon the mistakes of the past. We remember our failures when we should recall our victories. But even in the abyss that has swallowed us, we may remember that there is strength in the Lord.

"Hear my cry, O God,/and heed my prayer;/from earth's far end I call to thee,/as my heart faints./When troubles are too strong for me,/do thou direct me" (Psalm 61:1−2, Moffatt). *Amen.*

The Will to Live

March 6
Isa. 55:3a

Our whole being struggles to surmount the difficulty. We realize that others depend upon us; we must live because of them. Our faith must remain sure. We cannot let down our family and friends. In the past, others have helped us; we have helped others. We cannot give in to this trouble. We are needed. We are important. Slowly strength presses in and we begin to question our despair of yesterday.

Why am I so sad?
    Why am I troubled?
I will put my hope in God,
    and once again I will praise him,
    my Savior and my God (Psalm 42:5, TEV).

NEW PATHS OF THE SPIRIT — March 7
Ezek. 36:26

We begin to realize that life can never be the same again. We do not feel that we are the same person we were. Not only does life seem different but sights and sounds have taken on new significance. Music has greater depth. Words of scripture and poetry suddenly carry meanings that touch our inner being.

People become very important to us. We feel the heartbeat of the stranger. The masquerade by which we lived is shorn from us and we emerge a new person.

I waited patiently for the LORD;
he inclined to me and heard my cry. . . .

He put a new song in my mouth,
a song of praise to our God (Psalm 40:1, 3, RSV).

THE NEW LIFE — March 8
Isa. 42:5—7

"I the Eternal have called you of set purpose/I have taken you by the hand,/I have formed you for the rescuing of my people . . ." (Isa. 42:6, Moffatt).

This new life is fed at its source by our concern for others, a greater respect for ourselves, and our openness to the love and pain of those with whom we live.

It is to share your food with hungry men,/and take the homeless to your home,/to clothe the naked when you see them,/and never turn from any fellow-creature./Then shall light dawn for you,/with healing for your wounds. (Isa. 58:7—8a, Moffatt).

No longer shall we equate good health and freedom from trouble as marks of God's approval. Rather, we shall grasp good health as a gift to be cherished and used creatively.

THANKSGIVING March 9

Psalm 116:12

I will sing and praise you!
Wake up, my soul!
Wake up, my harp and lyre!
I will wake up the sun!
I will thank you among the nations, Lord!
I will praise you among the peoples! (Ps. 108:1b−3,
TEV.)

Out of the overflowing heart the words of praise burst forth. We feel relief that good health can be a reality. That which we most feared has not happened. Growth and understanding have emerged from worry and struggle. We know a deep, abiding joy. We have been tested by fires and torments and have emerged unbroken.

I will praise you in their meeting:
People not yet born will be told:
"The Lord saved his people!" (Psalm 22:22b, 31, TEV.)

Irene VanBoskirk, Chevy Chase, Maryland

Available Power • March 10−16

March 10

Matt. 26:36−46

Christ taught the secret of receiving power from his and our heavenly Father in the garden of Gethsemane. His first prayer was, Not my will but yours be done. Two wills were clashing. He returned to his disciples and found them sleeping. Upon returning to prayer, his request was different: Your will be done. No longer two wills, only one. Power to forgive his disciples, power to withstand the betrayal, the scourging, the thorns, yes, even the crucifixion was given him, because he had surrendered all. This is the secret. Only by complete surrender to God's will do we receive unlimited power to meet the opportunities of service and the vicissitudes of life.

Father, I come just now in complete surrender. May your will be done through me for your glory.

March 11

Acts 9:1—8

The study of Paul's life reveals again that power comes only in full surrender. Paul had deep convictions—convictions that Christ was a mere man and not the Son of God. Thus with a clear conscience he persecuted the Christians. But when he met Christ face to face on the Damascus road, he surrendered all to him. This encounter brought two questions from Paul. Who are you? And what do you want me to do? Paul did not hesitate to obey the directions given him.

In studying his life, we find that power was bestowed on him to witness, in many places and under diverse circumstances, to the lordship of Christ, to his forgiving love, and to the availability of power to overcome.

God, so fill me that I may be your messenger of power.

March 12

Acts 8:26—36

Here is another example of power following surrender. The eunuch was reading but not understanding. Philip made the scripture alive and applicable to the eunuch's needs, witnessing to the good news of Jesus and his way of salvation. As the chance presented itself, the eunuch asked that he fulfill Christ's requirements. Again power and joy followed surrender. We have heard again and again Christ's invitation and his promises. Many of us have mentally accepted but have kept reservations in our hearts. There can be no barriers between us and God's will for us. Parents, life partners, children, money, social positions, and personal ambitions must all take second place.

Father, just now accept all of me—my life, my desires, my will. Fill me with thy Spirit.

March 13

John 15:1-8

For the last three days we have looked at biblical examples of surrender and power. Today we want to consider Jesus' promises to us. The Bible is full of precious promises but most demand some action on our part. Jesus, in discussing discipleship before his death, burial, and resurrection, says we must be as close to him as the branches are to the vine. The life-giving elements of a vine must traverse the vine to reach the branches. All parts of the vine work together to produce new growth, rootage, and fruit. Our power must come through Christ. His promise is based on the premise of our abiding in him. Would you be a part of the vine or just a brush pile?

Dear Lord, may I, this day, surrender to thy will and abide in thy love.

March 14

Rev. 3:14-22

The people of the church at Laodicea thought they had all they needed. Their leader did not find blemishes on them but the Spirit's dislike was so great that he wanted to spit them out—to break all relationship with them. Why? Because they were lukewarm—no fire of enthusiasm, no heat of commitment, no channeling of the power of God. Let us this day examine ourselves and determine the heats of our desires. Do we really care when anger, hatred, unconcern block the power of God? Are we really concerned when we fail to witness to his all-consuming love? Do we ask forgiveness?

Forgive, Father, my lukewarmness, my failure to clear the channels so that your power may flow through me. Just now, I open the channels. Use me.

March 15

1 Cor. 9:24—27

Paul has told how hard it is to do good, how often we know what is right but do evil. Remember how Peter Marshall prayed in the Senate that God would help us know what is right but help most when we know what is right and don't want to do it.

Let us examine ourselves. What do we really want? God's will for us? Stop—listen for direction. Are we relying on God's power? Surely we want to be the bakery that dispenses the bread of life, the aqueduct that channels the water of life, the cable that carries the light of the world. But are we limiting God's power? In Psalm 78, the psalmist recounts the failures in Israel's life. He concludes that the people failed because they limited God's power.

Just now, Father, give me power to follow your leading.

March 16

Deut. 33:25—27 (KJV)

God has not promised us a life of ease. He has not rolled out the red carpet. He has promised that life will be so hard that we will need shoes of iron and brass. But he also promised that underneath are the everlasting arms and that as the day so shall our strength be. As we see the injustices of the world, we know that we do not need to solve them alone. For God has said all power is his.

Praise, prayer, and expectation are vital to receiving power. Praise affirms our love and willingness to obey. Prayer formalizes our requests in words. Expectation confirms our faith. Power is the gift received.

Fill me, use me, lead me to the needy places to show others your great love and power.

Mrs. T. V. Hubbell, Lincoln, Nebraska

Reaching Out • March 17—23

REACHING OUT TO PRAISE GOD   March 17

Rom. 15:1—6

". . . Everything written in the Scriptures was written to teach us, in order that we might have hope through the patience and encouragement the Scriptures give us. And may God, the source of patience and encouragement, enable you to have the same point of view among yourselves by following the example of Christ Jesus, so that all of you together, with one voice, may praise the God and Father of our Lord Jesus Christ" (Rom. 15:4—6, TEV).

We may have to overcome many obstacles to be in church on Sunday—sleepy children who need motivation, a sports enthusiast headed for the greens, or the usual aches and pains that slow us down.

But whatever the difficulties, we all need to reserve a special time together each week to praise God.

REACHING OUT TO OTHERS   March 18

Phil. 4:13

Monday mornings in my household are all alike. The house is a mess. Decisions must be made and this involves a close look at the calendar. Priorities must be established.

A quiet time with God usually helps to ensure a smooth-running day and a week that includes the sharing of many Christian experiences.

When I consider the time bracket for having my hair done, I'm always alerted by the question that comes to the surface so loud and clear, "What time are you allotting to reaching out to others?"

Never has God needed our help more in this area. The daily witness I see of others reaching out is a source of strength to me.

REACHING OUT TO UNDERSTANDING   March 19

Prov. 3:5

The unspoken thoughts we have in a given day often include some like these: Why did that happen? What caused her to do that? What made him say that? Simplified they read, Why that?

The accumulation of knowledge we obtain from living a number of years is in itself a treasure. But a mistake we often make lies in not updating the knowledge properly. This day can be exciting, if we rely more fully on God's help in understanding our life.

First, let's reaffirm our faith in him and know that he is with us. Second, let's pray for guidance in reaching out beyond ourselves for a deeper understanding of God's love and power. Then we can be confident of growing also in our understanding of others.

REACHING OUT THROUGH ACTION   March 20

1 Sam. 2:3

Let me suggest that you locate this scriptural reference and read it. Your Bible is in the other room? I understand. "Just exactly where is *1 Samuel*? I haven't looked for it in a long time." It's in the first third of the Bible —immediately following *Judges*. . . . Or, perhaps you were given this devotional book but, at the moment, your Bible is . . . misplaced? I understand.

"Talk no more so very proudly,
  let not arrogance come from your mouth;
for the LORD is a God of knowledge,
  and by him *actions* are weighed" (1 Sam. 2:3, RSV, *mine*).

Many of us would agree with speakers or writers who say we are, by and large, a society overwhelmed by apathy.

Today, let's take some *action.* If you have located your Bible, you're already one step forward in reaching out.

REACHING OUT WITH HELPING HANDS — March 21

The concordance of the Bible I have used for reference has more than forty listings that refer to *help*, such as—in me is your *help*, *help* my unbelief, *help* us. I want to talk about one reference that seemingly gets very little of our attention as compared to the amount of thought we give to ourselves.

"Remember those who are in prison, as though you were in prison with them. Remember those who are suffering, as though you are suffering as they are.

"Marriage should be honored by all, and husbands and wives must be faithful to each other" (Heb. 13:3 −4a,TEV).

Agreed—the message is clear. Would we all agree on our responsibility to the prisoners? Would we all agree that the number of divorces is a sad truth of our age? Could we help in these areas by reaching out?

REACHING OUT TO NEIGHBORS — March 22

Today I'm suggesting that we consider our personal relations with all those who live close to us. I am referring to those in the same apartment complex or those who live in other houses on the block.

Frequently, I need to address myself to the necessity of being more open to others, if God is going to have an op- of advancing his kingdom and yet, if I fail to reach out to my own neighbors, how can they know that I care? my own neighbors, how can they know I care?

The twelfth chapter of *Romans* has helped me in every reading. I seem to understand more of its meaning each time I reread it. Until you have the time to read it again, keep this thought in mind—"Be aglow with the Spirit, serve the Lord" (Rom. 12:11b, RSV).

REACHING OUT TOWARD BETTER HEARING   March 23

Rev. 3:20, 22

One person out of ten has a hearing problem. To know persons who are deaf or hard of hearing is to feel concern for them, and our desire to communicate with them is sharpened by their desire to understand us.

All of us have a hearing problem as we try to listen for the voice of God. It is as we reach out to others that we hear and understand more clearly the words and actions of our Savior.

Much of what we hear today is just noise—noise—noise. Yet most of us are listening—trying to hear something that's helpful, hopeful, even heavenly. This is where we can all reach out by saying something worth hearing for all who can hear, will hear, and do hear.

Anice McGowan, Des Moines, Iowa

Known by Their Fruits • March 24−30

March 24

Matt. 7:15−20; Gal. 5:22−26

Jesus has said that we can know people by their fruits. A Christian isn't identified by beauty, wealth, talent, accomplishments, or pleasing personality but by the fruit that his life yields. What are these fruits? Paul lists them in Galatians—love, joy, peace, patience, kindness, goodness, faithfulness, gentleness, and self-control. But it isn't enough to identify and define the fruits of the Spirit—to study them as a scientist might study a specimen under his microscope. I want this harvest in my life. How do I go about developing it? If I struggle, surely patience will elude me; if I battle, surely gentleness will not be mine. Only if I continuously yield to the Holy Spirit will the fruits of the Spirit be continuously evident in my life.

March 25

Joy is God's abiding presence in my life. If I can communicate this gift of joy, then I have shared the most important part of myself with others.

Joy is like a tightly folded bud within me. If I enclose it in a walled garden to shield it from the world, I build a prison that shuts out the light of God's love. If I choose to keep it hidden, I am without love and the bud will surely wither.

If I have the courage to open myself to all that life brings—whether spring shower or summer storm—without self-conscious cultivation, the bud will burst forth into a glorious flower for all to enjoy.

March 26

Peace is the knowledge of God's eternal concern for me. With this knowledge I find serenity even when life's daily activities boil and churn about me. Though the pace in this technological world is hectic to the point of frenzy, I find within myself a deep well of tranquillity that flows out through me to create an island of peace around me. When I communicate with God constantly, our home becomes a haven—a sanctuary from the wars that surround us. Knowing that I am his creation, I can view myself not with complacency but with creative realism. I can see my worth as a human being and recognize my faults without despair. Knowing I am his, I can reach out to others without fear. I can make myself vulnerable, trusting him for perfect healing of any wounds I receive.

March 27

Patience is the willingness to surrender *all* of my life to God's will. Do I really yearn for the gift of patience in this impatient world? In this age of doers, when one is rewarded for action (often in spite of its results), do I sincerely wish to be long-suffering? I often act without thinking, without praying, without caring. I often try to force the maturing and ripening of my faith—and yet I want no hothouse flower that withers if exposed to sun and rain. Frequently, I have selected a red, succulent-looking tomato from the grocer's bin only to be dismayed at its lack of flavor and texture. If I live without patience and neglect to keep constant, instant communication with God, perhaps I will be as disappointing as fruit forced into premature ripening.

March 28

What is the love that is promised as fruit of the Spirit? Is it the rapture of passion I find in my husband's arms? The rush of affection that sweeps over me when I see my children? The security and contentment I know when I am surrounded by my family? Or is it, more simply, the growing sense of Christian concern I feel for every individual—the growing recognition of every person as God's creation and precious beyond measure?

The more completely I open myself to Christ, the more eager I am to share him with others. I want to develop this God-given capacity for loving and communicating love. If my love is truly Christlike, then surely there will be a few less hungry, less naked, less lonely among God's children.

March 29

I claimed the gift of gentleness, at least partially, years ago when I discovered that in working with a rebellious, frightened child the best breakthrough technique is a gentle, firm touch. The child who jerks away in anger, who seems to feel violated by the slightest physical contact, is the child who most desperately needs attention and love. As adult children, we pull away from God's gentle touch. We reject gentleness in ourselves and others in spite of our need of loving forgiveness. When Christ reached out and touched people—both literally and figuratively—with a gentleness born of strength, troubled souls and bodies were healed. He still reaches out through all those who have the strength to develop the fruit of gentleness.

March 30

John 15:8

Faith is both the root of the plant and the fruit that it bears. To live a Christlike life, one begins with a seed of faith, a simple belief, a tentative trust—and faithfulness begins to sprout and put down roots. Every day lived in the sunshine of God's love strengthens and nourishes this plant. As the branches develop, they may be buffeted by the storms of temptation and sorely pruned by trials but as long as the roots remain healthy, there is the promise of fruit. Unlike the plant that bears only one kind of fruit, the harvest of a faith-filled life is a myriad of blessings—love, joy, peace, patience, gentleness, goodness, faith, humility, and self-control.

Dean Draper, Nowata, Oklahoma

Growing • March 31–April 6

GROWING FROM INFANCY   March 31

Babies are sweet and cuddly things. How often would we keep the infant tiny, with his grasping fists and husky cries!

Yet the baby can't stay small. The legs must stretch; the diapers go; the bottle must soon give way to vegetables and meat.

The baby never thinks of lying still, inert, ungrowing. He pulls and pushes, focuses and grabs in growing motions of his very own.

What, then, of us? Have we forgotten how to pull at pens and cribs that keep our minds stale and confined? Do we attempt to struggle with a toy we've named a problem? Do we stretch to clear away the dust and prejudices from a shelf that has needed cleaning for years?

GROWING AS A CHILD   April 1

It's spring now in the elementary school and all the very little people who came to the first grade in September with scrawny legs, too-big dresses, and fears of cafeteria lines have miraculously grown up.

The legs are longer. The dresses fit (though the boys' raincoats are still too big). And in the lunchroom lines, these very little people juggle trays of orange juice, milk, and barbecue with the expertise of connoisseurs and acrobats combined, while I move so clumsily that my half-filled coffee cup erupts upon the Harvard beets and sogs my sloppy joe. *They* have grown in height and skill and self-assurance.

Have I grown even just a little, Lord?

Growing in Marriage April 2

A marriage is more than sleeping, frying eggs, and looking for a new car together. It's more than charge accounts and children's shots and a camping trip every other summer.

Marriage can no more stand still than heated popcorn, two-year-olds, or mice. Marriage is not for enclosing in a white Bible or a safe deposit box or the trunk of a car. It can't be kept safe when put away or hidden, like a squirrel's nuts cached away for the winter.

Marriage is for honing, tuning, and growing. It can stand unintentional bruises better than moody silences. A marriage is for growing in ideas about open housing *and* Little League—for growing in activities like barbecuing *and* prayer.

Marriage is for sharing and for love.

Growing Out of Boredom April 3

Sometimes the days are just plain dull, Lord, when the sky looks heavy, when visitors are bored and I am boring, too, stifled by women's magazines and windows that need washing. I need to stretch and grow.

A kind of gray mood settles upon my sink and coffeepot and heart, saying, Why bother? And, Blah!

These moods sweep in like the ocean waves I've almost forgotten so far inland here in Illinois—but they *will* ebb. That is the single joy, the hope, the candle in the shadows of routine. Tomorrow, or this afternoon, or now, Lord, the gloom will dissipate, the phone will ring, a child will laugh, or an idea will be conceived and I will climb out of my chrysalis—out of my dull cocoon.

I shall stretch and smile and grow.

GROWING IN KNEE-BENDING   April 4

I would grow in knee-bending. Had I bent my knees more often in October, I should have more tulips blooming in May. Had I bent my knees more often, my kitchen floor would not be so dull now.

Those who bend hearts in daily prayer are those less devastated by the tragedies of life that bring bowed heads to the strongest and to the most frail of women.

Knee-bending may not always be in a lovely sanctuary. It may, instead, be while scraping garbage after a fellowship supper; listening to the rambling story of an old, wheelchair Christian; preparing a CWF lesson when you'd rather be playing bridge; teaching when you'd rather sit; listening to five-year-olds when you're tempted to talk.

May we bend our knees and hearts more often, Lord.

GROWING TOWARD DECISION-MAKING   April 5

Shall I wear my black jumper or my plaid wool? Shall I unfreeze the chicken or the meat loaf? Shall I go to the PTA or stay home and read a book?

My decision-making apparatus is getting rusty. It runs haphazardly. It can't make up its mind whether it is set to be a mother, a wife, a teacher, or a dodo bird.

That's the trouble about decision-making in the first place. You have to know where you're going before conscience, your Bible, your brain, or whatever decision maker you employ can tell you how to get there.

When in one evening I try to write to my aunt, make fudge for my husband, hem my daughter's skirt, and grade my pupils' papers, my decision maker gets its wires crossed.

Help me guide my life and my decisions, Lord. *Amen.*

GROWING IN ANGER   April 6

Make me more angry, Lord. Each year it becomes easier to stay in my rut, my pew, my comfort and not be ruffled by the world.

Wake me from the lulling satisfaction of middle age. Help me see that there are more things to be created than afghans and crewel pillows. Challenge my brain; distract my numbness. I ask this of you, Lord, yet I know I ought to be demanding it of myself.

Injustice flaunts itself about me and only occasionally do I raise so much as an eyebrow. Now is the time, soul, to survive—to rise up from inertia. Be strong! Be upright! Be angry with Asian hunger and ghetto poverty!

Be unsilent and uncomfortable for a start!

Bernice Hogan, Abingdon, Illinois

We Know the Words ... Give Us Lives to Match • April 7−13

April 7

Holy Week begins. The Rider comes! He weeps over us. But he doesn't shrug his shoulders and walk away.

> Once no people, now God's people. Once dead, now alive.
>
> Lost, now found. New being. More than we are!

We know the *words*. Give us *lives* to match.

Ah, Christianity, you wonderful, inside-out, upside-down thing! We don't have to climb to a certain height of goodness before we reach our Lord. It's not at the end of the Way we find him. "I *am* the way, the very place under your feet right now. The road begins as low down as you happen to be. Even if you're in a hole, the moment you set your face in the same direction as mine, you are walking with me." No wonder we call it Good News. God Is! Rejoice! This is our sin—to know the best and seek the second best.

April 8

What am I giving up for Lent? My CWF group! Give it up to Christ or else these 40 days come and go and leave us where we were—holding on to the illusion that all the troubles bugging us right now are due to somebody else.

The church is the Body of Christ. *Tuesday there will be an important meeting on table decorations.* The church is the instrument of God's will. *Family night will feature highlights from the Bowl Game.* The church is absolutely indispensable. *In June all activities will end until fall.*

Seek first the kingdom of God and all this will be yours! Is not the reverse true—that if we don't seek his kingdom, the opposite will move in on us? (And yet, the gospel would never have lived for me without the nurture of the church. Thank you, God, for my university and my powerhouse!)

April 9

When Mark Twain's second child, Susy, died, he said that her death was like a man's house burning down. It would take years to discover all that he had lost in the fire. I walk away from endless CWF retreats and assemblies seeing all that is lost as I watch those outside doors swallow you women up. And a whole world crying out . . .

Sure you do good works. When you change "what *can* I do" to "what *must* I do," the joy is gone. Do it with no conviction and you get no blessing! We confused Americans! We envy the sinners their fun and the saints their glory, and we're somewhere in between—not enough religion to keep us from misbehaving and just enough to keep us from enjoying it when we do.

Not even God can change the past. Only today is ours.

April 10

If we make a beginning, the rest will come. Our blessed sisters, back there in 1874, believed the Lord helped those who helped the Lord.

Livingstone in Africa got a note from the mission organization in London, wanting to know if there was a road to where he was working. Two men wanted to come and help him. Livingstone sent back word, "If they need a road, tell 'em to stay there. I need people who can come, road or no road."

Life is still uncharted for us, too. We won't find our way all marked and known with no chance of getting lost.

This I know—we can endure almost anything if we believe that our experience has meaning beyond the present moment of pain and despair. Nietzsche rightly said, "He who has a *why* to live for, can bear almost any *how*."

April 11

Took, blessed, broke, gave! Do this in remembrance.... When you remember Jesus, what do you remember?

That table is at the front of all churches. Not for decoration, not for resting, not for conferences, not a place to stay. It is for eating, but not for our own sakes only. We prepare ourselves to *do* from here what Jesus began at a rough table in Nazareth and one in an upper room.

I come to his table this night, where my risen Lord is breaking bread. So much I cannot understand, so much I cannot believe. But here, this moment, my body finds peace. It even likes me. My soul loves the Lord and I will go from here a walking arrangement of the "Hallelujah Chorus." Oh, nobody will understand but the angels (and they'll be busy with the music!)

April 12

He died today. Or twenty centuries ago or will die tomorrow. I "see through a glass darkly" (1 Cor. 13:12a, KJV) but in some way I know his death makes all the difference, for everybody, until the end of time.

Let us fold our "hammer hands" and pray. The hands that held the handle of the nail-driving hammer at Calvary are still here. *Our* hammer hands today crucify goodness, love, integrity, because we think we have better answers. Let us remember ourselves and ask forgiveness.

We do not despair; one of the thieves was saved. Neither do we presume; one was damned. We bow, thankful for the grace of God—that Power that breaks in upon our lives from beyond us. Get down on your knees and thank God that we don't have to earn, win, deserve, or merit it.

April 13

Saturday, the day of waiting! This is the in-between time—between Friday when men did the worst they knew to Jesus and Sunday when God proved this is still his world!

We seem to be waiting. In these times, when every day is the anniversary of something awful, why do we not see that Calvary is not a lesson in dying but the clue to living? The only reason is to *love* unconditionally and give ourselves to love in every relationship.

They still come to betray with a kiss, arrest in the night, and put away in the day. But the *only* way to handle evil—the only way to confront hate—is with loving and the giving of ourselves for the good of others.

Mary Louise Rowand, Dallas, Texas

Easter • April 14–20

April 14

Luke 24:1–12

One night in India, I was walking to our house from our neighbor's in the dark. Earlier we had seen a drunken man lying in the dirt in front of the gate. Upon hearing footsteps, I immediately imagined that the drunk was after me. Utterly panicked, I scraped my legs across the porch and beat on the door trying to get in. If I had only turned around, I would have seen my mystified neighbor behind me.

Aren't we all, at times, like the women at the tomb? If we'd turn and face our fears and doubts, we would find the known much less fearful than the unknown. Each such experience would help us face the future more confidently. We would gradually learn what it means to live by faith, being neither the women fleeing in fear from the tomb nor the apostles who passed off their words as an idle tale.

April 15

John 20:11–16

One day I was visiting in the home of one of the older members of our congregation. I noticed that many times during our conversation she called me by name. As a result, our talk was warm and personal.

Each one of us likes to hear our name spoken. Often we can even tell how another person relates to us by the way he or she says our name. Is it so strange, then, that Mary, deeply grieved, recognized Jesus only when he spoke her name? All questions became answers when he said that one word, "Mary."

The Good Shepherd "calls his own sheep by name and leads them out . . . and the sheep follow him, for they know his voice" (John 10:3–4, RSV). Do we hear God when he calls *our* name?

April 16
Luke 24:13—33

Every time I rode a train in India, I had the feeling that half of India suffered from some eye disease. Large white cataracts that formed on the outside of the eye lens were disturbing to look at. What a thrill to watch Dr. Rambo slip a special knife under those ugly masses and lift them off, granting sight to the blind. This seemingly simple operation gave new life to many.

If only new spiritual insights could come so instantaneously. But, like those with cataracts, we often have to wait until the darkness is complete before the light can strike. Yet we, too, are given new life when the revelation comes. Surely this is the kind of sight Jesus desired for us when he was sent "to proclaim . . . recovering of sight to the blind" (Luke 4:18, RSV).

April 17
John 21:20—23; 1 Cor. 12:11

Leslie, what's it to you that I have other things in store for Ashley? Isn't it enough to take notice of the work *you* have been given and the favors that have been bestowed on you? Don't you have enough to keep you busy using your talents, without worrying about the other person's performance or rewards?

Jesus' reprimand to Peter is valid for us today. Jealousy of another's opportunities makes us think we have not received as much. Or, from a different angle, we are so proud of our own gifts that we exclude those who do not demonstrate their faith in the same manner, thinking them less "blessed."

Help me, Lord, to be about my Father's business, without hindering others who are trying to do the same. *Amen.*

April 18
John 21:15−17

I saw a man almost drown once.
The boat turned over and he fell
Into water thick with reeds.
And he wouldn't drop his gun.
We on the sidelines seemed powerless;
Then a calming voice began to call,
"Swim, float, rest, tread; don't give up!"
Persistently that voice,
For two struggling, exhausting hours,
Guided the man, now nearly gone,
Till, with one last surge, hand met hand—

Could this be the kind of loving, directing care Jesus meant when he said, "Feed my sheep" (John 21:17b, RSV)?

April 19
2 Cor. 4:1−6

The pressures—the sounds—the sights
  The whole world is changing so fast, Lord,
    how can we keep up?
    where do we hear your voice?
Men walk on the moon—
  but others still dig out a mere existence from the earth.
We lengthen lives—
  yet often prolong the agonies of death.
We pray for peace—
  but we live by violence.
We say we want all persons to know the love of God—
  but we reject those who practice it.
    O Lord, may our lives be the lights that shine out of darkness. In him who is our light. *Amen.*

April 20
Gal. 5:1, 13−15

Son of the Most High, help me know so assuredly who I am that I can be free. Help me lose myself more and more in you every day, so that less and less of my old, bound self ties me down. I know that dropping all the masks of pretense takes risk but that without risk I will never live the life you have promised.

O God, let me, like Jonathan Livingston Seagull, wing to perfect freedom above all earthly strife. Through your resurrection and mine may I know abiding love. Put within me a desire to share the truth with those who seek after it. In the name of him who is the author of freedom. *Amen.*

Judith Landry, Knoxville, Tennessee

Finding God • April 21−27

FINDING GOD IN SIMPLE THINGS   April 21

Finding God is difficult if we expect tremendous displays of action, blinding flashes of lightning. God can be found there but such things are few and far between. God is found in simple things like the smile of a child, the light of humor in the eyes of a widow, the kindness of a friend. He is found in the quick steps of those on errands of mercy, in the healing hand of the surgeon, in the firm hand of justice. God is found in the strength of a father, the gentleness of a mother, the love of a mate, the confidence of a child. God is found at the bridal altar, in the awe of seeing a firstborn, in the pain of seeing a loved one pass from sight. In life's common realities—God is there!

Father, make me more aware of your presence.

FINDING GOD IN A FATHER   April 22

Thomas Olin Slaughter—father, minister—1893–1972

He is no longer here physically, yet his wonderful spirit remains. The pain of separation is great but the legacy of love transcends this pain. This man knew sorrow and disappointment but, as a minister, he could give comfort and encouragement to others. He lived his faith every day and was devoted to the church. His dauntless belief in people was amazing; his love of life was contagious. He left behind sixteen "Timothys" and two grandsons preparing for the ministry. Thousands make a better witness because of having walked beside him, and a family gives of themselves for others because of his life. In my father, Thomas Olin Slaughter, I first met God.

Thank you, God, for men like Dad who help us find you.

FINDING GOD IN THE WOODS   April 23

A hike in the woods is a delight. The vast variety of trees and shrubs, of wildlife and insects, of textures, colors, and smells shows me the infinite creativity of God. I see the majestic oak and the delicate flower. I find fragile mushrooms of different shapes and colors and a gnarled old tree. I hear the cry of a diving hawk or the soft whirr of hummingbirds' wings. I see the white rump of a frightened deer or catch a glimpse of a tiny chipmunk. I feel the warmth of the sun or the coolness of the mountain stream, the softness of a bed of leaves or the sharpness of a rock. As I walk through the woods, God waits at every turn of the path.

Father, thank you for giving us this earth that only you could create. May my eyes be open to its beauty.

Finding God Through Encounters — April 24

I look deep into the eyes of another person in an encounter group experience. I see in her eyes a fear of revealing her true self. As our eyes are locked in a search for an inner "something," the fear slowly melts away. I see another being with hurts, mistakes, and sorrows, striving to be understood but afraid. I begin to see a soul emerge—bright, joyful, alive, and glad to be out of its prison. I see more—I see God!

God is within her just as I feel he is within me. I can see this same fact dawning upon her, also. We are forever akin because we have bared our souls to each other and have glimpsed our God in each other.

Lord, sometimes I forget that you are in each of us. May I see you in the next stranger I pass on the street.

Finding God in a Consecration Service — April 25

The scene of the consecration service at the CYF conference had been decorated for a party and we were the guests at what turned out to be the greatest party God ever gave for me. Christ's birth was *celebrated* with scripture and the singing of "Joy to the World." We read of the great love of God for us. We rejoiced in the story of the Resurrection. Party hats, balloons, and streamers were handed around. The "Hallelujah Chorus" rang out through the night. We shouted and sang our joy and our love for God. Sparklers in hand, we ran to one another saying, "I love you," with a newfound meaning. The Holy Spirit moved like an electric current through us. The openness was beautiful to behold. God was there!

Father, now I celebrate your life with new boldness.

FINDING GOD IN MY FRIEND April 26

She isn't a person who always serves through the programs of the church. My friend finds ways of serving in her daily work. She found an old widow without food and bought groceries with money out of her own pocket. Another house revealed an elderly mother—paralyzed—whom she encouraged to move again. In still another home lived a family without enough clothes; my friend brought them things to wear from her own home. Again and again, she gives.

A boy comes to her for hope because there is none in his own home to help him. Another boy finds in her a staunch ally in juvenile court. She finds time to comfort a friend who is grieving for her dying father. God lives in her heart and shines in her actions.

Father, make me more like my friend.

FINDING GOD IN EXPRESSIONS OF LOVE April 27

The small group of twenty persons gathered for Communion under the trees. Those who wished brought symbolic gifts to share—a jar of tadpoles showing new life, a blossom for a husband signifying a marriage relationship, a rock for a new minister, a handclasp for a new brother, twenty hand-tied knots to show our closeness, an expression of love from a boy with tears in his eyes, and two hands offered to show the tower of strength God can be.

As we were asked to find someone to give communion to, my heart throbbed because my nineteen-year-old son strode to find me. I found God that day in twenty human beings.

Lord, give me opportunities to open my innermost self to someone else, revealing you also.

Eleanor S. Kuss, Memphis, Tennessee

Reconciliation—How Do You Spell It? • April 28 – May 4

April 28

Recently I invited a friend to share in an important planning session on reconciliation. He took out his notebook and was preparing to mark the date on his calendar. With a puzzled expression on his face, he turned to me and asked, "How do you spell reconciliation?"

How *do* you spell reconciliation? Getting the fourteen letters put together in the right order to spell the word and learning how to pronounce it correctly is one thing, but knowing and practicing what lies behind the spelling is another thing. How do *you* spell reconciliation? I spell it love . . . forgiveness . . . concern . . . understanding . . . sharing . . . communicating . . . witnessing . . . action.

O Lord, your Son has set the example. Help me follow him. *Amen.*

April 29
Acts 17:26a

Over the past few years, I have discovered that the better acquainted I become with those of different cultures and racial groups, the more I realize that the desires, aspirations, and capabilities of the different peoples are much the same.

We who are followers of Jesus Christ—who believe in his gospel of good news for all persons—should be the first to realize this truth. But somehow we continue to judge people by artificial standards rather than as human beings.

Help me, O God, feel the power of love as it crosses all barriers, knows no boundaries, and favors no status or culture. May I truly understand that increasing my love of neighbor will increase my love for you. *Amen.*

April 30

One of the highlights of a recent visit to Africa was the opportunity to share in the closing session of a training institute for rural women. Our party of eleven had been transported to the center at Chalimbana, a short distance from Lusaka, Zambia, by a friend who had served with me on the national board of Church Women United when she was in the United States. During the welcoming remarks, the director of the center stated, "Your coming this long distance in order to learn of our program and to share with us *makes us feel like human beings.*" These words seem to be ever before me, calling to my attention the many inhumane acts that take place daily.

O God, help me reach out and touch somebody's hand, greeting him or her as a human being. *Amen.*

May 1

It is a rare but joyous moment when one witnesses sacrificial love. I had just shared in prayer with an elderly woman who was confined to her home with terminal cancer. She arose from her chair, went over to a cabinet, and took out two jars. Handing me the larger jar, she said, "I don't have much to give, but I have been saving my pennies. I will keep this small jar to purchase something for our bathroom when we get one. This is my 'others' jar. Please use it to help someone who is in need." Knowing of her devoted prayer life and her love for others, I placed her jar of pennies on the altar at a World Day of Prayer service the following week. The theme was "Bear one another's burdens" (Gal. 6:2a, RSV).

O God, help me learn how to live for others. *Amen.*

May 2

It is easy for most of us to have sympathy for others, particularly in times of sorrow, disaster, or special need. We send cards and flowers and make visits to express our concern. We view scenes of disaster and human need on television and read about the deplorable conditions at home and around the world. These touch us momentarily and our sympathy is aroused. But empathy is another matter. It means having such an interest in another person that you can place yourself or picture yourself in the other person's shoes and look at things in the same way. Few of us ever take the time to get close enough to another person to really understand a different point of view.

Help me, O God, to see the needs of others through their eyes so that reconciliation may take place. *Amen.*

May 3

1 John 3:18

"Make love your aim" (1 Cor. 14:1a, RSV).

It is one thing to think about being loving and friendly and another thing to express love. How does the world judge the sincerity of my life? By what I say I am? No. By the results of my life. G. K. Chesterton said on one occasion that nothing is real until it is local. But near-at-hand compassion requires the risk and cost of personal involvement. I ask myself where I am going to start and the answer is so simple that it frightens me. I need to start right where I am. Now is a good time—a right time—to begin.

Today may I find a need near at hand and become one of God's centers of action in the world. *Amen.*

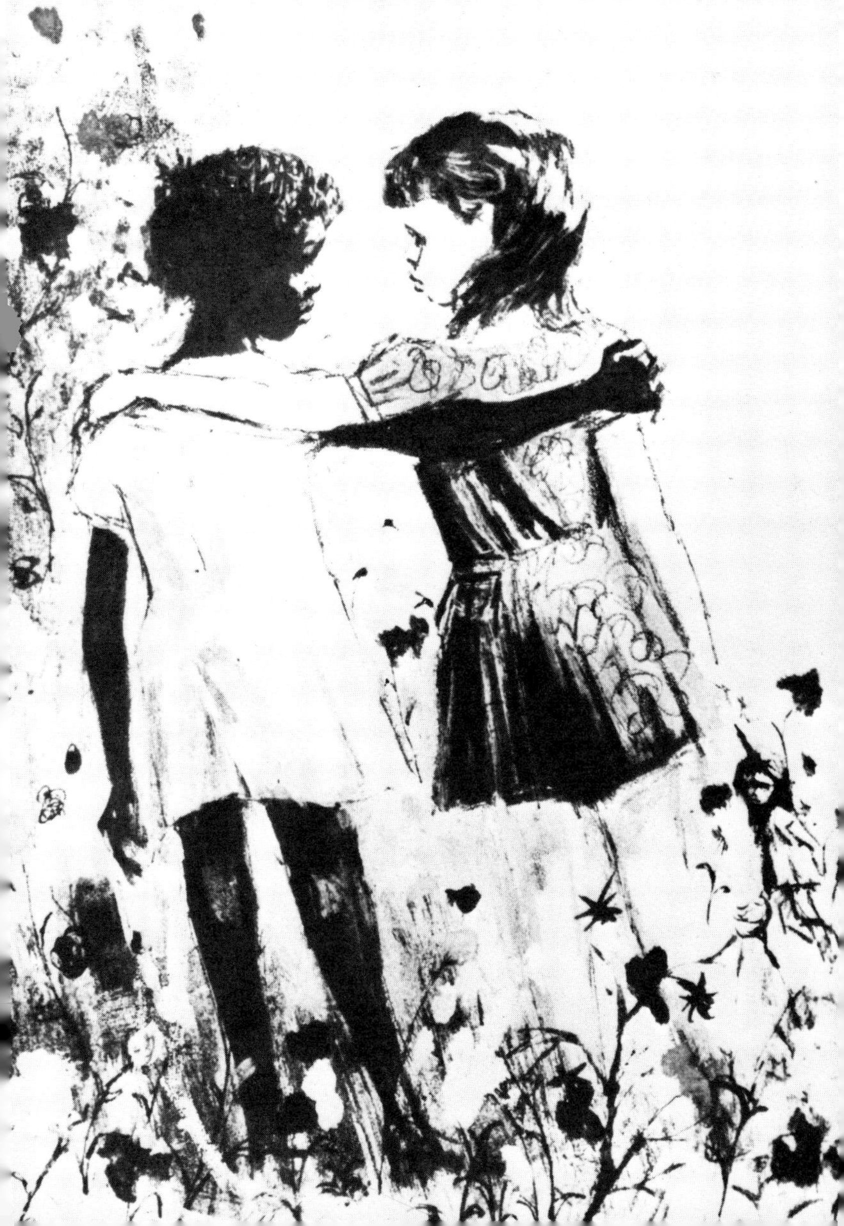

May 4

"Let each of you look not only to his own interests, but also to the interests of others" (Phil. 2:4, RSV).
At the close of this week, let me be honest with myself.
Am I really willing to give of myself?
Am I willing to make an effort to help other persons?
Do my neighbors know I am a Christian?
Do I take a firm stand against social evils everywhere I find them?
Am I honestly willing to accept all people and show them Christian love, regardless of their nationality, color, or race?
Am I willing to go the second mile?

O Master Teacher, show me the way. *Amen.*

Dorothy D. France, Pulaski, Virginia

Recipe for Love ● May 5-11

TAKE 2 HEAPING CUPS OF PATIENCE   May 5

The symbolism of two may be taken as God and Job. In Job, God reminds us that man is not the measure of his creation. The universe is immense, constructed on no plan or theory that the human intellect can grasp. It is transcendent everywhere. This is the burden of every verse and is the secret, if there be one, of the poem. Sufficient or insufficient, there is nothing more.

God is great; we know not his ways. He takes from us all we have; but yet, if we posses our souls in patience, we may pass through the valley of the shadow and come out in sunlight again. We may or we may not. . . . What more have we to say now than God said from the whirlwind more than twenty-five hundred years ago?

1 HEARTFUL OF LOVE   May 6

O Christ, I know how thou hast treated me—with forgiveness, gracious and undeserved.

Help me treat others with the same spirit. Only as thy Spirit takes the place of my old spirit can I do it.

Thou wilt outlive all that is contrary to thy love. For love is eternal; hate is of a passing hour.

I surrender myself to love—to love even where I do not like. For thou canst make me love the unlovely, and perhaps in the process they will become lovely. *Amen.*

2 HANDFULS OF GENEROSITY   May 7

The generosity of God is expressed in two words—condescension and clemency. This includes God's relenting from the strictness of his rights against us; his allowance for our imperfect righteousness; his remembering whereof we are made and measuring his dealings with us thereby. God demands of us the same attitude toward our fellows. (See Matt. 18:23—35.)

Generosity is expressed in two great women. Margaret Beaufort, the gifted and learned mother of Henry VII of England, endowed the colleges of Christ and St. John at Cambridge. Anne Boleyn persuaded her husband, Henry VIII, to sponsor the first "official" translation of the Bible into English—the Great Bible of Coverdale.

1 HEADFUL OF UNDERSTANDING   May 8

There is only one Christian faith—the faith proclaimed by the apostolic preaching to which the New Testament bears witness; and this faith is expressed in the historic church. It is the faith of the whole church—the catholic faith. The modern sectarian association of the word *Catholic* is one of the ironies of history. Just as the same joy and peace in believing is shared by Francis of Assisi and John Wesley, Thomas Aquinas and John Knox, Martin Luther and St. Paul, so also the same essential truths of the faith are held by Roman Catholic, Methodist, Anglican, Presbyterian, Lutheran, Baptist, Greek Orthodox, and Christian (Disciples of Christ). Far-reaching differences, both theological and ecclesiological, exist and may not be minimized. But, fundamentally, we all share the same historic faith.

SPRINKLE GENEROUSLY WITH KINDNESS   May 9

Remember the three levels of life and decide on which one you are going to live.

There is the level of life where you return evil for good—the demonic level; the level where you return evil for evil—the human, legal level; and the level where you return good for evil—the Christian level, the divine level.

If you give evil for good, then you become evil—you become the thing you give out. If you give evil for evil, you become a tit-for-tat person—legalistic, unlovely, and unloved. If you give good for evil, then you are born of the good—you become good.

ADD PLENTY OF FAITH AND MIX WELL   May 10

This instruction portrays the joyous, exuberant, exciting young author, Anita Bryant. Her book *Amazing Grace* is a personal witness to the fact that God can really transform ordinary people when they accept Jesus as Lord and Savior. Anita plunges into the pressures, the rigors, the tensions, the sheer panic of mixing her family life with all her professional activities into one homogeneous blend—all the while trying to stay in one piece, with health and sanity intact. Her Christian faith, reinforced by her husband's deep personal faith and his love for her, has filled her with an amazing grace, so powerful and fulfilling that she has been able to do things she never thought possible.

I recommend that all women read this book.

SPREAD OVER A PERIOD OF A LIFETIME   May 11

There's a web that's been weaving for centuries—
White hands flitting back and forth
Over a tissue of darkness, weaving in legends and lies,
Which small, white minds have viewed gladly
And felt themselves growing in size.
It's grown and it's grown for centuries—this tissue,
This web, this lie—but must it keep on forever?
Our hands are strong in their blackness.
They can tear the web into rags.
They can find the light lost behind it—
Find a new day and a promise of justice—
Find goodness and love and the real whiteness
Of liberty, brotherhood, right.

Eunell Pouncy, Denver, Colorado

Family Relationships • May 12−18

May 12

Prov. 31:28a

In a centennial year, it is not enough to honor the women of the past. We need to think a bit about what gave them their inner strength and how they were able to transmit their convictions to others. I have come to realize that the woman who was most successful in transmitting her values to me was my own mother. The idea frightens me a little. For I begin to ask myself, What philosophy of life have I passed on to my daughters? And what are they passing on to theirs? Mother never called me to her and said, "Daughter, here are some eternal truths I want you to hear." It was her personality and the way she faced opportunities and problems that influenced her daughter.

O God, we pray that we may be worthy of the Christian heritage that is ours. *Amen.*

May 13

Prov. 31:27a

My mother believed that homemaking was a challenging career and could be one of the most creative and satisfying careers open to a woman in any era. She believed it was just as important for a homemaker to acquire professional skills as for a nurse or a teacher. For that reason, she encouraged her daughters to major in home economics—nutrition, child development, money management, and family relationships. She gave me the feeling that homemaking is more than being "just a housewife." It is a challenging profession and a creative one. It is being a co-worker with God.

We are grateful, our Father, that you have trusted us to share with you in the joy of creating and nourishing life. *Amen.*

May 14
1 Tim. 4:14a

My mother believed it was important for people to have confidence in their own abilities. She saw each of her eight children as a distinct individual and was able to make each of us feel important. She went to school plays, debates, and athletic contests. She respected individual differences and encouraged each of us to develop special interests and talents. In her busy schedule she even found time to tutor children with reading difficulties. In later years she received letters of appreciation from men who said, "Your help was the turning point in my life. You made me feel that I *could!*"

Eternal God, help us encourage all those whose lives we touch to feel more confidence in their God-given talents. *Amen.*

May 15
Deut. 6:6—7

Mother (with Dad's help, of course) was able to create a climate in which we had fun and enjoyed one another. There was never enough money but somehow it never occurred to us that we were poor. We all learned to work—we had no choice. I realize now that much of our heritage was transmitted to us in the discussions we had while we picked strawberries or shelled peas. Today it is more difficult for families to have these opportunities for sharing work and wisdom. Occasions differ but the rewards are the same. We have to work at it a little harder.

Forgive us, Father, when we do not make the most of the rare occasions when we are together as a family. Help us see their potential in forming attitudes and in building memories.*Amen.*

May 16
1 Cor. 3:6

My mother believed that parents' responsibilities were to provide opportunities for growth and to cultivate a desire for it. Realizing the difficulty of financing a college education for eight children, my parents moved from a rural community to a university town when the oldest child was through high school. By their providing room and board and instilling in us the incentive to achieve, we all received a university education. When the youngest graduated, we felt that our parents should have been awarded an honorary degree. They had faith that God would use their efforts in helping their children grow.

Keep us, God, from wanting to do more and more *for* our children. Give us the insight to see that we help them only as they learn to do without us. *Amen.*

May 17
Psalm 23:1

My mother's faith in God and his purposes helped her meet crisis and heartache nobly. When a pilot son lost his life in the service, she made us feel that we must each contribute a little more to life to make up for the life that was lost. In her garden she had a rosebush named for each of us. On her kitchen windowsill, one morning, was a red rosebud, fresh with dew. "That is Hubert's rose," she said. "It makes him seem very near." Her faith in immortality was expressed in a tangible way through a scholarship loan fund named for the son whom she had not really lost.

God of love, we thank you for the assurance of your help in time of trouble and for the lives of those who have witnessed to that truth. *Amen.*

May 18
John 10:10b

My mother's conviction that maintaining a meaningful husband-wife relationship was essential to creative home building was once expressed in these words, "Dad is even more important to me than are you children. I had him before I had you and I hope to have him many years after you have left." That wish was granted. They were blessed with sixty-two years together. When we voiced concern about their driving to Florida each winter, Mother retorted, "If you get word that we have been killed in a car accident, don't grieve for us. Just know that we have been having a good time all along the way!"

Our Father, help us praise you and rely upon your promises every day of our lives. *Amen.*

Edith R. Evans, Austin, Minnesota

Becoming a Sensitive Christian • May 19−25

A GLUM OR GLORIOUS FACE

May 19
Eph. 5:9−10

"Everyone . . . saw Stephen's face become as radiant as an angel's!" (Acts 6:15, Living Bible.) I believe my face can reveal something of my inner spirit. I hope it can show love, joy, peace, kindness, and strength.

A child, sick in the hospital at Christmas, heard of Jesus for the first time. She wanted to share this Good News with her nurse, who told the child that she had heard that story. The child replied, "You have? I thought you looked as if you hadn't." The curious nurse asked how she looked and the child's answer was, "Oh, kind of glum like most folks."

"Create in me a new, clean heart, O God, filled with clean thoughts and right desires" (Psalm 51:10, Living Bible).

A TOUCH OF FAITH   May 20

James 1:2—8

A census taker finds out much about each of us. I'll try being my own "senses" taker.

I wonder if my sense of touch is attuned to my faith so that when trials and suffering come (as they surely will) it can sustain and purify me. I recall the woman who had faith to believe that a touch of the Master's garment could heal her (Luke 8:43—48).

My daughter was told after surgery that the growth removed was malignant. I have seen her mature in thought, live each day with gratitude, and become a source of strength to family and friends. We have seen "a quiet growth in grace and character" (Heb. 12:11b, Living Bible).

Lord, I pray for faith for today. *Amen.*

SENSIBLE, SENSITIVE SIGHT   May 21

Eph. 6:6—8

A person went to the mountaintop. When asked what he had seen, he replied, "A potato bug."

"A sensible man watches for problems ahead and prepares to meet them" (Prov. 27:12a, Living Bible). I believe that hindsight is good; it makes me grateful for those who have gone before me, providing a map for study and guidance. I must also have foresight and dream of a better tomorrow, as well as the insight of work for today to make the dream a reality.

In a vision Isaiah saw the Lord and heard him asking, " 'Whom shall I send as a messenger to my people?' " (Isa. 6:8a, Living Bible).

Lord, give me a sensible, sensitive sight. Help me see more than a potato bug at my feet. *Amen.*

GOOD HEARING   May 22
                                      Prov. 15:31—32

"O my people, listen to my teaching. Open your ears to what I am saying" (Psalm 78:1, Living Bible).

Before her firstborn arrived our niece expressed the fear that she would not hear her baby cry at night. I assured her that she would, for her face, voice, and eyes revealed loving concern. She asked why I was so sure and I replied, "Because you'll be listening!" Later she told me that I had been right.

Most of us would not be tempted to pick up our neighbor's purse and carry it home with us, but have we ever "picked up" some damaging gossip that we repeated and thus stole our neighbor's good name?

Lord, I need help to become a good listener and use wisely the things I hear. *Amen.*

BECOMING DIET-CONSCIOUS   May 23
                                        1 Cor. 3:1—3

Paul gives us some good advice: "You have been Christians a long time now, and you ought to be teaching others, but instead you have dropped back to the place where you need someone to teach you all over again the very first principles in God's Word. You are like babies who can drink only milk, not old enough for solid food. And when a person is still living on milk it shows he isn't very far along in the Christian life. . . . He is still a baby-Christian! You will never be able to eat solid spiritual food and understand the deeper things of God's Word until you become better Christians and learn right from wrong by practicing doing right" (Heb. 5:12—14, Living Bible).

Lord, give me a taste for more than baby food. *Amen.*

RELEASED FRAGRANCE   May 24
                                            2 Cor. 2:14−17

"As far as God is concerned there is a sweet, wholesome fragrance in our lives. It is the fragrance of Christ within us, an aroma to both the saved and the unsaved all around us" (2 Cor. 2:15, Living Bible).

No matter how costly and fragrant the bottle of perfume, it is of no value to me until the seal is broken and its fragrance can be released. I must learn to release fragrance or love to others in many ways, like a bouquet of sweet peas whose varied shades and colors all send forth the same sweet smell.

I am told that Luther Burbank worked for twenty years to give the dahlia a "pleasing fragrance." I must not grow weary and discouraged.

Lord, show me new ways to express my love. *Amen.*

COMMON SENSE   May 25
                                            Psalm 92:12−15

"Have two goals: wisdom—that is, knowing and doing right—and common sense" (Prov. 3:21a, Living Bible). Wisdom tells me that God loves me; common sense says the best way to show my love for God is by becoming sensitive to the needs of others—trying to be a taste of salt (Matt. 5:13) that makes a difference. Paul must have thought of folk like me (seventy-plus) when he wrote: "So take a new grip with your tired hands, stand firm on your shaky legs, and mark out a straight, smooth path for your feet so that those who follow you . . . will not fall and hurt themselves . . ." (Heb. 12:12−13, Living Bible).

Willetta Park, Bargersville, Indiana

Varieties of Service but the Same Lord • May 26–June 1

May 26

Phil. 4:13

Though our family had often traveled in Canada, still it seemed strange coming across the U.S.—Canadian border to live in Canada as "landed immigrants." Immigration agents were kind and helpful, and clearing customs took less than two hours. But our family was emotionally exhausted as we drove on into Ontario, where my husband would assume a new pastorate in a new country. We pulled over to the side of the highway where, amid the traffic, we asked for God's guidance and strength in this new life.

We all have moments of insecurity, such as moving into a new community, meeting new people, or just trying something we have never tried before. But it is good to know that we can look to God for guidance, companionship, and confidence. God gives us the strength we need.

May 27

Eph. 4:1–6

Grocery shopping in Canada was a new experience. Salt, oatmeal, coffee, and shortening, which I had always bought in round containers, were now in square boxes or even bags. Many brand names were different and, because Canada is bilingual, all labels were printed in both French and English. As I confronted a variety of containers, I was reminded of people and how we differ. We certainly do not all look alike; we live in different surroundings and speak different languages.

Yet as I opened these "different" containers, I discovered that the contents were much the same as those I had used in the States. So it is with Christians. How much alike we are on the inside, when we have accepted Christ in our hearts and worship the one God and Father of us all.

May 28
2 Cor. 5:20

"What do you think of that, Yank, eh?"

This was the greeting received by our daughter following one of her history classes when the teacher had made some very harsh judgments of the U. S. and its policies.

During a Woman's Day service, I referred to our daughter's experience. Following the service, two retired teachers approached me. One took my hand and said, "Let us apologize for that teacher and assure you that his attitude is not ours."

Probably unconsciously, this woman was taking the role of an ambassador. The work of an ambassador is to dispel antagonism and open the way to reconciliation. It is the Christian's privilege and responsibility to be an "ambassador for Christ."

May 29
Acts 10:34—35

We stood in a Canadian church on Canada's Dominion Day, holding our Sunday bulletins. On the cover was the United States flag, for in the U.S. this was Independence Sunday. Our children held their church school papers filled with pictures and references to U.S. history. This experience sharply illustrates how often we give religious credence to *national* symbols and celebrations in an *international* church. God is not exclusive. He is not American, nor Canadian, nor Irish, nor African. He is not the friend of one nation only. Through his Son, Jesus Christ, God revealed his all-inclusiveness.

O Father, keep us all from pride of patriotism that forgets that Jesus Christ is our true King. May the peoples of the world unite into one great family serving the Lord. *Amen.*

May 30

Rom. 12:9—15

The wedding was lovely and now the bride and groom were welcoming some 200 guests to their wedding reception. Speeches filled with appreciation and good humor followed the dinner. Then the bride and groom, carrying baskets of individually wrapped wedding cake, walked among the tables, presenting the cake and thanking each guest for sharing the joy of their wedding. The happiness of our first rural Canadian wedding was contagious.

Joy is to be shared. Dozens of little joys and some big ones come our way each day. The joy of beauty—a flower, a sunset, or a walk in God's world; the joy of creativity—an apple pie, a gem of verse, a thoughtful note; and most important, the joy of our faith in Jesus Christ. Joy will multiply when truly shared.

May 31

1 Cor. 3:5—7

Our small country church, like many other churches across Canada, was beautifully decorated with pumpkin, squash, corn, apples, peppers, and tomatoes. It was the second Sunday of October, Thanksgiving Sunday in Canada.

We sang with grateful hearts as we looked upon this evidence of God's bounty. This was a celebration of cooperation with God. These people had prepared the ground, planted the seed, and cultivated to make the best possible conditions for growth. Then God had given the increase.

So it is with the Christian life. Conditions are not always ideal. Our work is not always what it should be. Yet our responsibility is to make the best use of what is available. If we work in cooperation with God, he will give the growth.

June 1

Eph. 2:19—22

People often wonder how it feels to live in another country. Where is our allegiance? We are U.S. citizens and proud of our homeland, but we have come to love this great country of Canada and its people. This love might be likened to love for our children. We love our first child so dearly and yet, as a second is born, we find that the love in our heart has grown enough to include this new child. The curious thing about love is that there always seems to be enough. Christ opens the way and becomes the bond in every new relationship. We never love our country less when we love Christ more. We are just living by a larger allegiance. In Christ we are no longer strangers.

Joyce Leland, Wainfleet, Ontario, Canada

Saying "Yes" to Self Brings Life • June 2—8

IT'S THE MORNING OF YOUR LIFE

June 2

John 16:33

Dear Lord,
It's the morning of my life!
There is much for me to learn,
   much for me to experience; yet I'm old
     because life has already brought me through so much.
Childhood, adolescence, maturing years,
   marriage, and children. Days filled with laughter, joy,
     love, tears, sorrow, loss, friendship, anger, hope,
       wondering, wishing, pain, frustration, and caring.
My feeling is all filled up! And yet you say to me:
"Look! See! Grow! Do! Be! It's just the beginning!"
   I wonder about it, Lord.
     I have a feeling
       that morning will last forever. *Amen.*

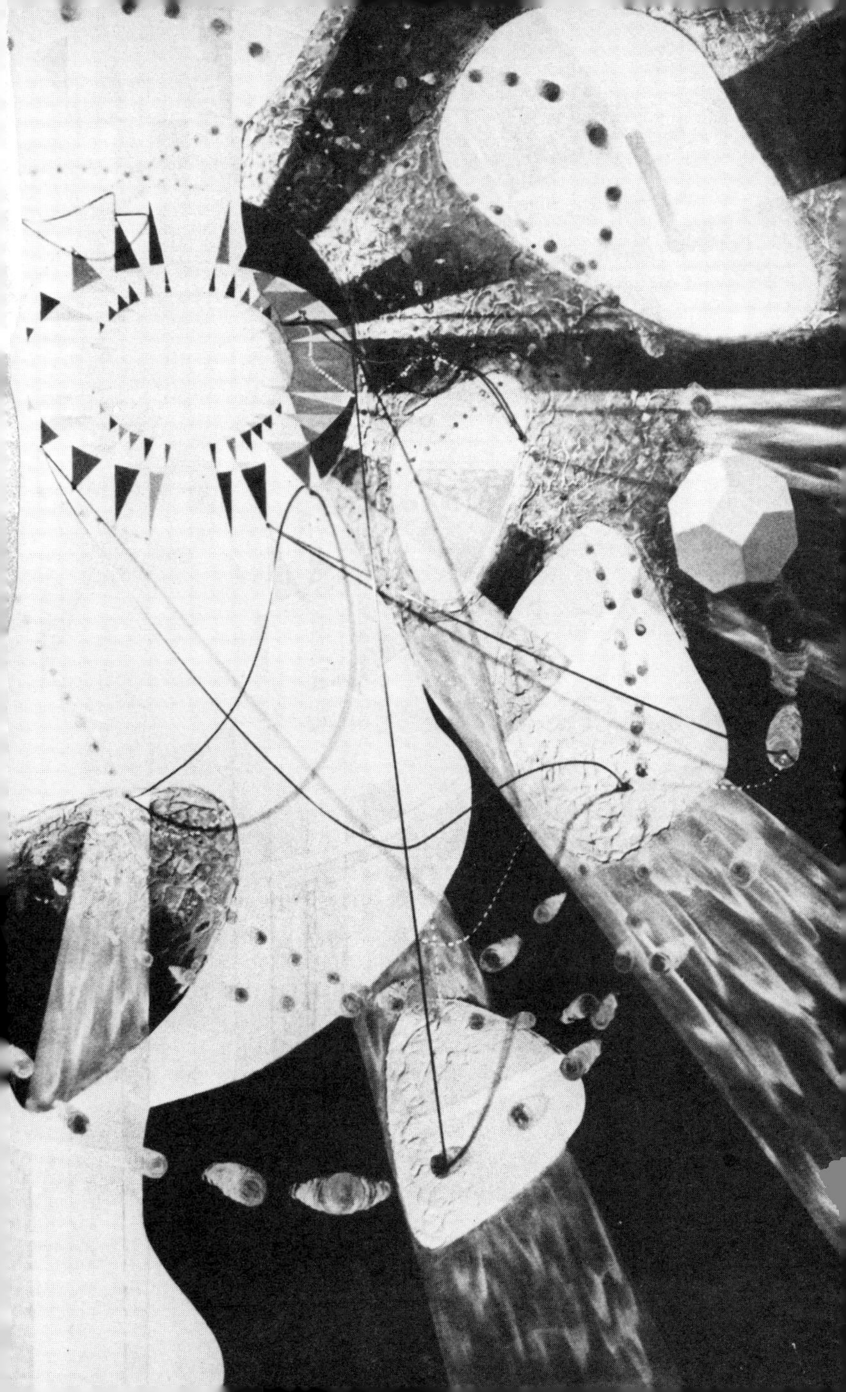

ALONG THE WAY   June 3
TAKE TIME TO SMELL THE FLOWERS   Psalm 8:3−9

Many of God's miracles are small. Our days are filled with the clutter of living. Sometimes it is difficult to wade or see through the litter in order to experience the small miracles by which life is made rich. My memory goes back to the many walks I took with my children when they were young. In the midst of the hassle of a huge city, suddenly they would squat down oblivious to the clatter around them and with bright eyes and chubby fingers fondle the tiniest, colorful weed. Much of our ability to experience God's creation is dependent upon the pace we choose for ourselves in living.

Dear Lord, thank you for my moments of aloneness with your creation. Open my eyes to the little/big things of life. *Amen.*

BLOOM WHERE YOU ARE PLANTED   June 4
                                                             Mark 5:25−34

This slogan calls us to learn to live life with spontaneity, to give and receive openly what life brings to our doorsteps. We are sometimes so busy looking afar for a place to serve that we miss the opportunities of love and witness that are within reach of our very hands. Jesus didn't have to make plans to serve people. He walked into the midst of the life around him to love, affirm, and share with those whom he met. It's a matter of living life fully. It's letting that light shine from God through us to others and through others to us. God's gift of caring relationships is a precious gift indeed.

Dear Lord, show us how to be open to the possibilities of our lives. Let us know the Spirit within ourselves. Show us how to serve and receive where we find ourselves. *Amen.*

FRIENDSHIP DOUBLES OUR JOY   June 5
AND DIVIDES OUR GRIEF   Gal. 6:2

Friendship is an integral part of Christian community. Often a sharing, caring community develops out of necessity. We've all experienced how calamity brings people together. The crisis provides a focus and calls us to work toward a common goal. For Christians, God's gift of community provides a springboard to daily living. Out of both the difficulties and joys of our lives we are together—we are one in the Spirit. We need not look for this to happen only in crisis or in heaven, for there is a fantastic *now* to Christian faith—a now that calls us to the thrilling, expanding life of belonging to the Christian community.

Dear God, help us know that the kingdom is within/among us here. Let us share our lives with others. *Amen.*

JUST BE! IT'S ENOUGH!   June 6
                                Heb. 4:15−16

Be what? Be ourselves! But what/who are we? I am Eleanor, wife and mother, child of God. That is the part I'll let you see, but there is a part I try to hide—even from myself at times. One day I happened on John Killinger's book *For God's Sake, Be Human*, and I am indebted to him for his open, honest approach to living. He points out that the contrived self is a narrow, limiting one. Through the gospel we have been given the freedom to live openly and honestly before God and man. God's grace is wide enough to encompass all that we are—good and bad. Healing comes by trusting in God's forgiveness and then moving from that to learn to forgive ourselves.

Lord, help us understand ourselves and celebrate what and who we are totally, joyfully. *Amen.*

You Have Touched Me June 7
and I Have Grown Matt. 9:1−7

Today let us spend a few minutes thinking back to the times in our lives when our understanding of God was increased by a caring, loving person. Within the intimacy of sharing the heights and depths of our lives, we are given the opportunity to touch one another and build common ground from which all can grow. To share with another in Christian love is to invite each other to grow and to be the best of that within us. But Christian love and sharing is difficult. It means we must have courage and trust in order to remove our masks and be seen as we are—without pretense. We need to experience not only God's acceptance but our neighbor's acceptance and our self-acceptance—just as we are. When we are touched by a person with that kind of love, the gospel becomes real.

We Can Appreciate the Miracle of June 8
A Sunrise Only If We Have Psalms 139:7−12
Waited in Darkness

By experiencing a "wait in darkness," I received new meaning for my life. In 1971 I was severely injured in an accident and spent a month apart from the world—deprived of vision and the ability to speak. Out of my struggle to survive, I tapped the faith within me and found it alive and beautiful. The most memorable event was experiencing my death during a hallucination. I knew horror and fear but there was such joy in the victory that my comfortableness with death is now an important treasure.

I am convinced that to each of us, in its own time and way, life brings opportunities through which we can choose to grow/live. Let us be open to our life's lessons and choose to live through them to rich, full lives.

Eleanor Meyers Burchill, Lawrence, Kansas

I Am the Vine; You Are the Branches • June 9-15

June 9

According to the Scriptures, we are sons and daughters of God. "I ascend unto my Father, and your Father; to my God, and your God." (John 20:17, KJV) Seeking a personal relationship with Jesus, we accept his invitation, enter his family, and are called Christian but we often fail to listen or surrender to his will in perfect obedience. Then brokenness occurs.

Our peach tree has a strong trunk with a sturdy branch up the middle, to which hundreds of small branches are attached. The center branch bore big, juicy peaches; the others bore tiny, juiceless fruit. A storm broke off most of the small branches and nature's pruning helped the whole tree bear wonderful peaches. So it is with our tree of life; brokenness need not mean separation from God but an opportunity through new growth to serve him in obedience.

June 10

While camping among the pines of the White Mountains, I became lost only a hundred yards from camp. Fog had closed in behind me and I lost all sense of direction. I reacted with a frantic call to my husband. When he answered, I cried, "Keep on answering me, so I can find my way back."

As Christians, we often walk in a fog, heading in the wrong direction, lost and wanting God's answering voice. If we are sincere in listening and do our homework, we find that Christ has given us an outline of behavior and a goal not beyond our attaining. He calls us to follow the path with discipline, faithfully committing to him our love, our time, our money, and our soul, as we shout "Yes" through the fog.

June 11

There are many ways for us to seek the presence of our Lord—ways that will help us look into his face, enable his love to enter us and make our spirits radiant. When I see, say, or think *tree*, I think *God*, and all kinds of worship experiences open up to me.

By an irrigation ditch in Arizona, standing alone, is a huge, gray, gnarled, old cottonwood tree. It seeks life beside this man-made stream. At first glance, one would say it serves no purpose in living. It is too far away from the road for one to sit under but it has served many a traveler as an altar to God because of its beauty and majesty against the clear Arizona sky. Our souls experience God in these moments of spiritual exaltation while viewing such beauty. Praise God for his creation.

June 12

On a cloudy evening, as we rounded a curve toward home, we looked off to our right toward some mulberry trees and saw the sky black with starlings. They seemed to know about the coming storm. All were darting and tumbling through the air, screeching at one another, needing rest and trying to land in the trees. It was devastating to watch, for we could sense panic in the darkening sky.

I was to remember this sight many times when overindulgence and darkness would creep into my life. But in my quiet time, Christ would open his everlasting arms, dispelling frustrations and fears with a warm glow of love. Darkness turns to light and I am rested and ready to travel the curves of life in deep thankfulness for divine fellowship.

June 13

Last summer our son, aged ten, wanted to build a tree house in our front yard. A few of his friends came to help, only to get bored with the project and quit. But he received wonderful help with the framework from his brother-in-law. Boards and nails were handed up to him by Mother. Father encouraged him and checked for sturdy construction. Big Sister brought out cold drinks and Little Sister made curtains. Later, when it was finished, his friends liked what they saw and joined him, spending many happy hours by day and night in the tree house.

Heavenly Father, may the services we render and the concern we have for others be so Godlike that those around us will like what they see and join us in the Light.

June 14

When I was a young mother with a very sick child, fires of prayer were kindled in the hearts of fellow sons and daughters of God and we felt the sparks of love. Our Lord gave us a miracle. Our family has been the happy recipient of strength through intercessory prayer in various crises in our life. Because of these experiences, I have become a serious disciple of intercession—of losing my *self* in prayer for others.

Intercessory prayer is not hesitant or half-hearted. It is like tossing logs on the fire with all our strength. It is the agonizing use of all our fuel—mind and body. Let us gather in our thoughts those to whom life has dealt a hard blow and offer them before God as bright sparks ascending from the flame of our prayer. Let the Holy Spirit carry our supplications to the Father. We must expect miracles.

June 15

Walking up a wash from the lake, always looking for beauty in driftwood, I found in my path a large piece of gray wood, half hidden under debris. I unearthed it and took it home with me. Cleaning, polishing, sanding, waxing, and caressing it were pure joy. Our lives, like that piece of wood, are sometimes hidden under debris—sin, despair, temptation, defiance, greed, ego, fear, weakness, and self-righteousness.

Father, cleanse and polish our spirits with promise, forgiveness, generosity, and love. When we are sanded down with repentance, humility, purity, and faith, we accept your caress. Our broken, troubled hearts are filled with the triumphant, redemptive power of Jesus. May our lives be the eloquent expression of pure joy. *Amen.*

Jody Vanderkolk, Tucson, Arizona

This Is the Day ● June 16−22

June 16

This is the day which the LORD has made;
  let us rejoice and be glad in it. (Psalm 118:24, RSV.)

In these precarious times, I do not cease to wonder that God has given us one more day in which we can praise him, witness to his love, and grow in his grace.

How are we going to use this day that he has given us? Will we forget that he is near, that he is waiting to be acknowledged in our thoughts, our prayers, our words, and our actions?

I pray that we may rededicate this day to him, that we will lean on his everlasting arms and let him guide us through the hours that lie ahead.

June 17

Last summer, a tragedy struck a family we know. A young mother, her five-year-old son, and her mother were killed in an automobile accident. That fateful evening, as we gathered around the television set, hoping to hear the story was not true, we prayed that God's will be done. Finally, the newscaster announced that the tragedy had indeed happened.

"Oh, Lord," I prayed, "I can understand the taking of the two women, but, Lord, why a five-year-old child?"

For just a second, I saw two women with a small boy running across a beautiful field. I could hear the familiar laughter of our beloved Jimmy Joe, and a feeling of peace came into my heart. I ceased to question the wisdom of God, for I knew they were all happy.

June 18

One of the finest Christian people I have ever known was a man in our neighborhood who devoted his retirement years to the growing of flowers and vegetables.

Each year his love for God was reflected in the colors and hues of his flowers and, during many worship hours, our sanctuary was graced by blossoms from his garden.

As he worked among his flowers each morning, he whistled a hymn. His afternoons were spent reading his Bible and, before his eyesight failed, he had read the Scriptures completely through three times.

His life and his dealings with all revealed the true meaning of this verse:
"This is the day which the LORD has made
    let us rejoice and be glad in it" (Psalm 118:24, RSV).

June 19

"For the LORD sees not as man sees; man looks on the outward appearance, but the LORD looks on the heart" (1 Sam. 16:7b, RSV).

Our Father, we thank you for showing us the truth of this verse. In this day of changing life-styles, we see the Spirit working in mysterious ways in the hearts and lives of many of our young people. We see them bow in adoration and complete submission to your will. If each of us could forget self and be willing to love one another with the enthusiasm of youth—if we could forget petty differences and overcome the hardness of our hearts, O God, what a beautiful world we could leave to our children.

We do indeed thank you for this day which you have made; may we have the courage to rejoice in it. *Amen.*

June 20

I once read a short meditation telling of a young girl who couldn't attend worship in her church on Sunday because of her working hours. But during the intervals of her work she spent her time in prayer, asking God's blessing on the brides and bridegrooms of that day, the newborn babies, the families of those who had died, and the problems of the world as a whole, as these were reported in the daily paper.

Do you need an inspiration for prayer? Read your newspaper and remember by name before God the people you read about each day. You will soon learn what it can mean to pray without ceasing.

Let us rejoice in the opportunities God gives us today, and may we realize more fully the power of prayer.

June 21

One day, after many sleepless nights, I went to our family doctor to get some pills. To my surprise, he refused to give me any. Instead, he gave me some advice that I have found relaxing and money-saving. And when I awake, I am well rested and refreshed.

"When you find you can't sleep," he said, "get up, dress warmly, and read your Bible. Since you can't sleep anyway, what difference does it make how long you read? I guarantee it will work."

It does work; I challenge anyone to try it. However, remember, before you begin reading, to call upon the Holy Spirit to guide you; put all that troubles you at the foot of the throne; then read. Remember also to thank God for his presence and comfort.

June 22

In a recent study of the life of the Apostle Paul, my intermediate class discussed his stay in the Arabian desert after his conversion.

It occurred to me that we, too, have deserts to cross—times when we are so busy with our daily routines that we do not spend enough time communicating with God through his Word.

Travelers crossing the desert stop at an oasis for refreshing water, food, and rest in the shade of the trees. We, too, can find an oasis of spiritual water with which to quench our thirst and food to satisfy our hungry souls, if we but stop, rest in God's Word, and then find someone to whom we can be of help.

Alma Schooler, Buhl, Idaho

God Is! Rejoice! • June 23–29

I WANT YOU, LORD! June 23

I'm running and hectically busy in the kingdom, Lord. It really is yours, when I stop to think. Most of the time I act as if it were mine. When I stop dead and think, I recognize my deception and become afraid. I really want you in my life, Lord. I want to shout, sing, and rejoice in the sure knowledge that God is. But how?

In Persia a boy asked his teacher, "How can I find God?" His mentor took him to the edge of a pool, bade him bend over, and pushed his head firmly under the water. Finally he released the boy, who gasped, "Why did you do that?" His teacher replied, "Only when you want God as much as you wanted air will you find him."

I want you, Lord. I am empty. Fill me. Fill me to over-run-n-ning with you. I'm ready, Lord. Now! *Amen.*

I'M ON MY WAY June 24

I'm celebrating today, God, with guitars twanging a new melody, balloons cascading in a fresh breeze, with fireworks cracking and humans reaching out and touching in love. Why yesterday was I empty? Why? Didn't I know that you have been part of me since I was? Today I *know.* I don't know how. I just know! I'm a new creature reaching out in joy and hope. I'm strong in the faith today.

Oh, I'll weaken. I'll forget that I'm me and you're you and I'll mix it up again. But I think I'll remember more often now, for inside me a seed is rooting. And I'm not alone. I've been touched by an endless march of women past and I'm being stirred by hands and spirits of others who have invaded my being. They are in me, even as you are, and together we move forward. O Lord, I'm on my way today!

YOU AND I LORD   June 25

I've been thinking, Lord. All that running around I was doing in your kingdom for them. All that me! I surely was on an ego trip. Biofeedback tells me now that it wasn't me. It was really *You—in me*. Why didn't you make me face it? Why did you let me think I was so good and helpful? I *am*? O Lord, how can you so gently and powerfully accept and love me? If I could do all that on the level of just feeling it should be done for others, how tremendous it could be when you and I do it together, with me knowing I give that cup of water in your name! That loaf of bread I share is in your remembrance. That word I speak is but a replay of your voice. The sacrifice I make is but a small imitation of your vast act. Together, Lord, we are going ahead now in your kingdom. Together. Now!

I'M IN THERE TRYING   June 26

What a breakthrough, Lord! I'm a different person. Know where I am? I'm down below the decks helping man the pumps that suck out the water threatening to sink our ship. Up on deck they are singing; the band is playing; the sun is bright. I work hard, for it seems as if we settle lower and lower. I tried to tell them up there but they laughed or were embarrassed. So I labor here and not alone. A host of us scurry around, working at every spot that seems to be weakening. Above the noise we sing and rejoice, for we know that you are in this ship, too.

Someday, Lord, *someday* . . . after we have subjugated space and computerized all our dilemmas, we will stand naked, barren, despairing, desiring, and seeking and there will come on the flood of Creation an *eighth day*.

How, Lord? June 27

I find it is becoming hard to identify myself. I'm perplexed and often confused. Lord, as a corporate being I turn, revolve, and spin between being Martha who kept blocking Jesus, Mary smashing social patterns, Prisca risking her neck, Lydia establishing a house church, and the woman at the well stirring up a whole city. I am many, Lord, but how do I take my uniqueness and fuse it into the ever-moving, ever-freshening stream? I seem to be reaching out so far that the ground beneath me swells and rolls. Help me, Lord, to keep alert, seeking to know your will for me as I move out in my greater supportive role in your kingdom. Keep ringing in my ears your counsel, "Stand firm in one spirit, with one mind striving side by side for the faith of the gospel" (Phil. 1:27b, RSV).

I Drink and Drink June 28

"Everyone who drinks this water will be thirsty again, but whoever drinks the water that I shall give him will never suffer thirst any more. The water that I shall give him will be an inner spring always welling up for eternal life" (John 4:13–14, NEB).

O God, this is your world and you are flowing and moving in it surely, purposefully, and lovingly. I drink of you and venture forth in renewed faith in many streams, not knowing the end from the beginning. My sustenance is in you—expectant, fearful, exultant, impatient, and secure. My cup is so full that it is running over. Strange, I drink and drink and drink but it never seems to diminish! God, I know you are at work in me and I rejoice. *I rejoice!*

I AM, LORD! June 29

An ancient fairy tale tells of a king who had three daughters, each of whom gave him the gift she thought most precious. One gave him the rarest gem existing, another a golden palace, and the third, a mill that could produce salt endlessly. He disdained the humble gift of the third daughter and divided his kingdom between the other two. But one day, when no salt was to be had in his palace or his kingdom, he realized the love in that lowly gift.

I am the salt of the earth. I am a light shining in the world. I am all this and much more because you, God, are indwelling in my being. In joy, hope, and celebration, I delight in the gift of you in my life and in exultation I shout the Good News—God Is! Rejoice!

Virgi Reed, Topeka, Kansas

Human Liberation • June 30—July 6

HUMAN LIBERATION June 30

AND THE RICH James 1:9—11

In an America that boasts of being the richest nation ever to grace the face of God's earth, there are still brothers and sisters among us who have no share in that affluence. They are the ones we pray for on the World Day of Prayer and shower with old toys and clothes during the infectiously benevolent holiday season. They are not, however, our constant concern, as they should be. Are they not the ones whom Jesus told us to feed, clothe, and love? They *must* be our constant Christian concern, if they are to have their share in that affluence we so obviously exploit. The author of James says that the rich will pass away and the oppressed will come into the flower of full and final liberation. As Christians, we must aid in that process.

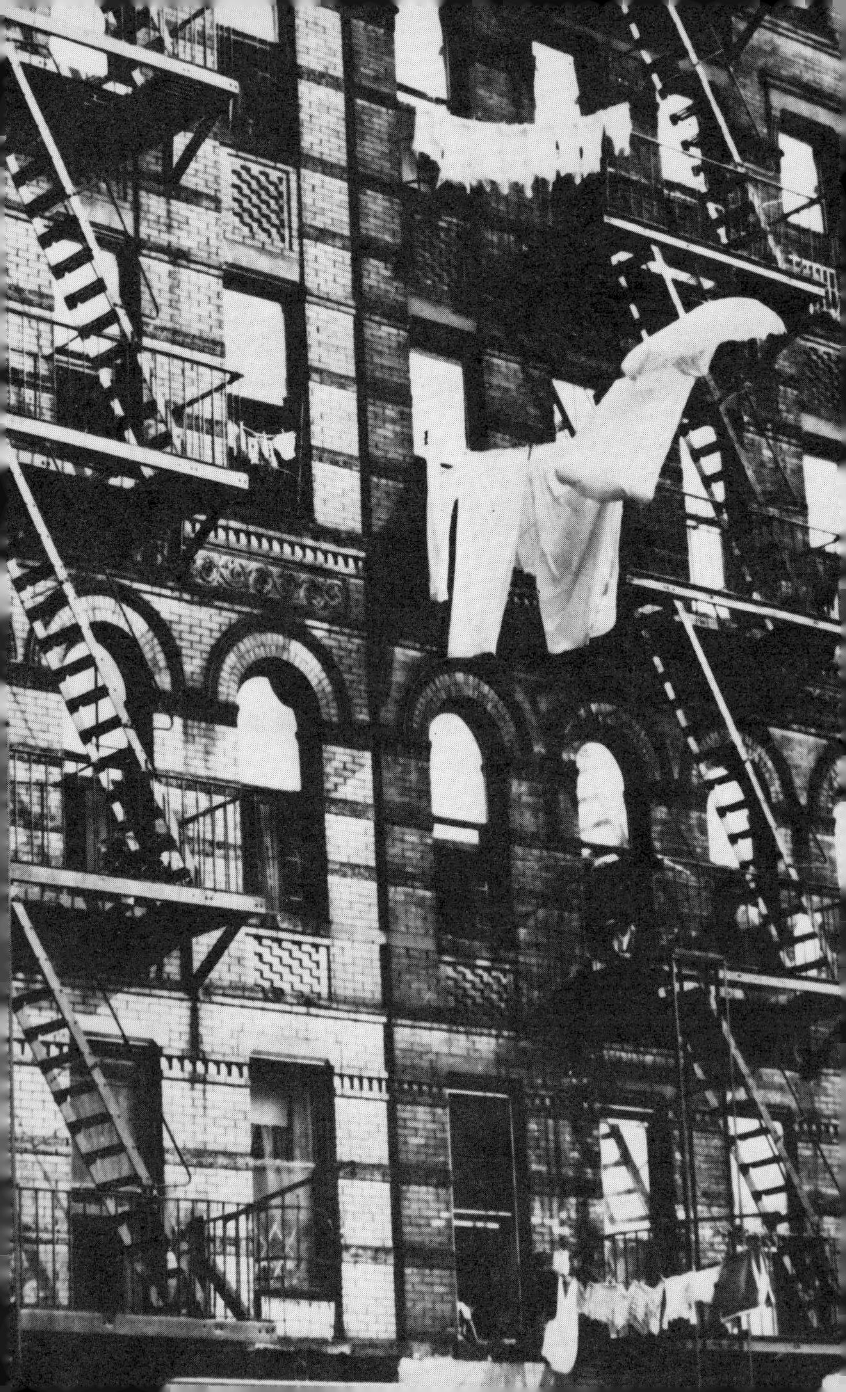

HUMAN LIBERATION July 1
AND PREJUDICE James 2:1–13

". . . you are guilty of creating distinctions among yourselves . . ." (James 2:4a, TEV).

The entire Book of James warns against the prejudice that plagues us as human beings. The ugly seeds of prejudice have become culturally ingrained even in those of us who claim to be Christians. The author of James warns us to love our fellow men and women as individual human beings and not to act in fearful prejudice against those who are not exact copies of ourselves. American white Anglo-Saxon Protestants have long been open and destructive in their prejudice. Christian WASP Americans can no longer create false distinctions out of God's natural equality for all people. God's judgment is now upon us. Our course of action is clear.

HUMAN LIBERATION July 2
AND THE ACTIVE FAITH James 2:14–17

"What good is there in your saying to them, 'God bless you! Keep warm and eat well!'—if you don't give them the necessities of life? So it is with faith: if it is alone and has no actions with it, then it is dead" (James 2:16–17, TEV).

This section from the Book of James speaks for itself. How can we say we love, if our actions fail to verify our words? Many of us have not only the necessities but also the luxuries of life. If we are satisfied to declare our faith and then promptly sit on it, our faith becomes meaningless. If our faith is not busy helping those who can't even boast of having life's basic necessities, then our faith is "dead." But our faith in action could liberate other humans.

HUMAN LIBERATION
AND THE ACTIVE TONGUE

July 3
James 3:1−12

The tongue has alwas been a problem of humankind. There are some people of all shapes and forms—male and female—who never really stop to think how dehumanizing their "harmless gossip" may prove to be. The author of James speaks plainly on this issue. He compares the tongue to a spreading fire that has no regard for those it burns in its torrid path. The language may seem a bit florid but the message is clear. The carelessly active tongue is often the most destructive, dehumanizing agent going. It could be the most liberating.

Next time, let us ask ourselves, "Is the story true, and, even if it is, what fellow human being may it hurt, if I repeat it?" before we begin to indulge in "harmless gossip."

HUMAN LIBERATION
AND WAR

July 4
James 4:1−3

Killing has been going on around the world for more years than any of us can remember. It seems that it is even second to nature to us now, for many of us do little more than sigh and shrug our shoulders as countries wage war on each other. We adhere to the false need of saving face rather than saving lives. We continue to kill in the face of the direct commandment, "You shall not kill" (Deut. 5:17, RSV). As Christians, we have a stance to take and we cannot ignore that responsibility by leaving such matters to diplomats and politicians who obviously need our help, judging by their records. War will never bring us what we want so desperately—peace, love, and liberation for all peoples. We must do more than pray for peace. We must demand it, for the sake of human liberation.

HUMAN LIBERATION   July 5
AND THE FARM WORKERS   James 5:1−6

"You have not paid the wages to the men who work in your fields. Hear their complaints!" (James 5:4a, TEV).

The migrant farm workers in our country are among the most blatantly exploited humans of our time. They are not able to rise out of their poverty because they are caught up in the ugly system that stifles their creativity with the agonizing hunger forced on them by the conditions under which they work. If ever humans needed liberating, these do. They deserve our constant concern and active campaigning for their final freedom. The Book of James warns Christians to hear the workers' complaints and to confront those responsible for the conditions that impair their natural desire for liberation from an unending poverty.

HUMAN LIBERATION   July 6
AND JUDGING ANOTHER   James 4:11−12

As we have seen, the Book of James is full of practical guideposts for Christian living. It lends itself to thorough and thoughtful meditation and insists on the realistic act of liberation. Perhaps no lesson in James is more important for us than James 4:11−12. "God is the only lawgiver and judge" (James 4:12a, TEV).

God did not give us the right to speak against any brother or sister. When we judge others, we take over the job only God has the power to perform. If we judge our brothers and sisters, we take the chance of making the awful mistake of being wrong. To judge others is to play God. Who do we think we are, to judge our fellow men and women?

Karen Warren, Fort Worth, Texas

Personal Relations • July 7–13

OLD FRIENDS REMEMBERED　　　　　　　　　July 7

Sometimes when we sit in church at worship, we hear a song or a specially worded prayer that reminds us of some beloved friend who has died. Our hearts are gripped with the remembering, as we recall the times that we have shared with them—good times and bad.

Our congregation was chartered just seven years ago and the older, experienced members who left their churches to start anew have occupied a very special place with us.

Their experience and patience, born of years of seeing things through, have brought a much-needed balance to our congregation.

God blesses us through the lives of his children and through our memories of them when they have gone.

Pray for the church and for all who serve.

THANK GOD, I CAN'T REMEMBER　　　　　　July 8

How often we cling to the old hurts—dragging them out, living them over completely, not forgetting a detail.

When the slur or the abuse has been perpetrated by a person of a race different from ours, we use the occasion as proof positive of "their" meanness.

I was talking with two of my co-workers and the conversation turned to women's liberation and racism. I remarked that I felt victimized more because of my race than because of my sex. I started to relate an incident in which I had been deeply hurt by an individual of another race. Then I realized that I had forgotten what had actually happened and who was involved. "I can't remember," I said. "Thank God, I can't remember."

Pray for ability to forget the hurts that come our way.

Only the Lonely
July 9

He was ill now, lonely and confined to a wheelchair. We had lost contact with him since he had married and moved away. A mutual acquaintance wrote that he asked about us often, so I wrote him a note. He called his friends to tell about his letter and the joy it brought him. He even called us to say, "Thank you."

I was ashamed for having done so little so late, and I resolved then and there to take the time to minister to him and to all the other people in like circumstances whom I knew, by calling, writing, and visiting.

Only the lonely know the real heartache of loneliness. We must share God's love with others. We must pray for the sick, the shut-in, the lonely. We must pray for the skill to minister to them in a meaningful way.

That's What Faith Is
July 10

I was driving to our home place recently with my sister, who was giving directions. I felt secure as long as I drove on the busy state highway, but when she said, "Slow down for a left turn," I became panicky because both sides of the highway were pitch dark. "Turn there," she said, "just this side of the white posts."

"But where is the road?" I asked. "I can't see a road."
"The road's there," she laughed. "Make the turn."

The road was there. After a moment, I said, "That's what faith is: believing, even when you can't see ahead."

If we would take part in meaningful encounter with others, we must move on . . . believing. The road is there.

Let us pray for the ability to be open, accepting and loving, even when we can't see ahead.

Because I'm the Teacher   July 11

I was a first-grade teacher for five wonderful years. The children were delightful and, although ours was not the quietest room, it was surely one of the liveliest.

The children moved about freely in our room, working and sharing. Whenever they had free time, they would gather in small groups and play "school."

One day, as we sat in the reading circle, I asked one of my most aggressive little boys, who was holding my pointing stick, to give the stick to me. He refused, saying he wanted it. I asked him again, and he demanded, "Why?" "Because," I said, "I'm the teacher."

Sometimes we must make decisions for our children just because we are the teachers or the parents.

Let us pray for the strength to "be the teacher."

You Are a Real Person   July 12

A young white teacher in our mostly black junior high school was having a rough time with a class of bright youngsters who found special delight in making her feel inadequate.

I promised to try to relieve the tense situation, but before I could act, I heard one of the students call out a cheery, "Hi! Miss X" to the teacher. I asked what had happened and she said, "Yesterday, I told them about the fights I used to have with my brother and about the terrible fears I had suffered and sometimes still felt. They looked at me and someone said, 'You are a *real* person.'"

Let us pray for the grace to be looked upon as real persons by all whom we encounter.

TROUBLED CHILD   July 13

I can see him now—scowling, hostility coming off him like sparks of fire. But in his eyes is fear—terror, like that of a frightened animal. The report says that he never got over his mother's death. He's lost, angry, and alone. Poor little black boy—thirteen and on his way to reform school.

O God! Why couldn't I reach him? Why couldn't I find the words? He wanted to break free. I know he did, but the urge to violence—cursing, fighting, destroying—kept coming back. I kept reaching but I couldn't touch him. O God! I couldn't touch him.

Let us pray for the children in the world who are lost, afraid and alone. Let us pray for the strength to keep reaching.

Estella Doty, Dallas, Texas

Ways of Loving • July 14–20

MY HEART IS FULL OF PRAISE   July 14

1 John 3:1; 4:16; Psalm 138

I thank you, Lord—
  for being so great that my mind cannot fully understand you;
    for your power. It is comforting to know that one tidal wave is more powerful than all the nuclear weapons men have made;
      for your boundless love—even making it possible for us to be your children;
        for the universe you created. You provided all the things we need, and you also made them beautiful;
          for enabling us to think, to work, to create, to worship, to share;
            for . . .

GOD LOVED FIRST   July 15
                                    1 John 4:7-8, 10, 19

"We love because God first loved us" (1 John 4:19, TEV). "This is what love is: it is not that we have loved God, but that he loved us and sent his Son to be the means by which our sins are forgiven" (1 John 4:10, TEV).

God, help me to get things in their proper order—to see this question of love in its right perspective. I cannot love you just because I decide to do so; I can love you only in response to the love you have for me. Your love is here, waiting for me to accept it. Help me open my mind, my heart, my entire being and allow you to fill me with the wonder of your love. Only then will I be able to love you perfectly, and only then can I love others as myself. What I have joyfully received, I will be able to give.

A MATTER OF LIFE OR DEATH   July 16
                                       1 John 3:14; 4:16

The commandment that is most prominent in the New Testament is the commandment to love—to love God and to love our fellow human beings. Because to love is to live. To live is to love. God is love.

"We know that we have left death and come over into life; we know it because we love our brothers. Whoever does not love is still in death" (1 John 3:14, TEV). This last sentence fairly leaps up from the page to seize our minds. It is said that the word *death* here does not mean a quick death—a single event—but a continuing, prolonged state of dying. And this is the condition of one who does not love. "Whoever does not love is still in death." But "whoever lives in love lives in God" (1 John 4:16b, TEV).

WHY DO I KEEP REMEMBERING? July 17

1 John 1:9; Matt. 6:14−15

God, I have been troubled again by memories of sins of the past. They lurk around the edges of my mind and interfere with my present work for you, even though I have long ago confessed them to you. Is this because I have not fully and freely forgiven people who have wronged me? I thought I had forgiven them; and yet I must not have truly done so, or I would not so often remember how they wronged me.

Please help me now, Father, finally to forgive those persons whose wrongs against me I still remember and to hold only goodwill for them. I want to do this not just in order to be able to receive and accept your forgiveness but because it is right that I should.

NO CHOICE July 18

1 John 4:20−21; Matt. 5:44−45, Luke 6:32−36

A Christian has many privileges, but the right to choose one's neighbors and one's brothers and sisters is not among them. Jesus made this clear in many of his teachings and in his life. We often draw the line between our people and other people, we and they, I and you. It is easy for us to give money, food, clothing, and books to be distributed by others to those in deep need. We find it much harder to deal directly with our brothers and sisters nearby. We don't want to be personally involved; we don't want to see the ugly need; we don't want to talk with or touch the one who is unattractive to us. We are embarrassed; we are conscious of our wealth; we feel superior. We are afraid . . .

Forgive us, Lord. Jesus did not feel so.

PERFECT LOVE DRIVES OUT FEAR   July 19
1 John 4:18

God, sometimes I am afraid to do things that your Spirit is leading me to do. I am afraid I can't do them well, or that I will be ridiculed or looked down on. I am afraid of what it may cost me in time, money, or energy; afraid of becoming involved.

Then I read, "There is no fear in love; perfect love drives out all fear" (1 John 4:18a, TEV). Help me remember that I am responsible only for faithful effort; results are in your hands. I have entrusted my eternal soul to you; why am I afraid to follow your leading in these small tasks?

I love you, Father, and I love my neighbors. I do not yet love completely, freely, fearlessly. But I love—Lord, perfect my love!

ENOUGH TALK;   July 20
ACTION, PLEASE!   1 John 3:18; 4:20−21; James 2:16

We were talking about teaching young children that what hurts them hurts others in the same way. One wise person said, "And when we have taught them that it hurts, we must teach them to *care* that it hurts." Most of the world's ills exist because we have not learned the second lesson. One who cares *does* something, The conference will not relieve Jimmy's hunger—but food will. The study will not warm Ann's cold body—but clothing will. Even our prayers unless we "put hands and feet to them" will not relieve suffering. If we think there are not enough resources or emotional or physical strength or time to care about the whole world, we underestimate the power of our God.

Let us pray actively and work prayerfully.

Dorothy A. Richards, Alpine, New York

The Worth of Each Person • July 21—27

July 21

Psalm 8

Twenty years ago, skirts hung almost to the ankle and we all wore them; when the hemlines were shortened, we followed suit. Then, a few years ago, skirts went back to midi-length but a majority of women did not feel the need to conform. Women were saying, "We want to wear what we like, not what someone else dictates." Today we can be ourselves in the style of clothing we wear.

"Do your own thing" is a popular phrase that suggests the feeling of many—"See me for what I am, a person unlike any other. Let me be me." A crying need in our highly complex world is for persons to be seen as individuals, each of infinite value, each a unique human being.

Let us pray that we may grow more fully aware of the uniqueness of each person.

July 22

1 John 4:20—21

If people want to be recognized as unique, even more widespread is the need to be seen as persons of worth. Mrs. Rosa Parks, riding the bus home from work one afternoon in 1955, decided she was just as good as anyone else and refused to give her seat to a white passenger. Hundreds of her black brothers and sisters in Montgomery, Alabama, sympathized; they, too, were tired of being treated as second-class citizens. From the protest of this one woman grew a mass boycott that triggered the modern civil rights movement. All over America black citizens demonstrated their demand to be seen as persons of worth. Why has it taken our country so long to begin to make things right? Let us pray that we may be used to help right the wrongs of our society.

July 23

Luke 4:16—21

It is a terrible thing to deny any person his or her full rights as a human being. Following the tragic events at Attica Correctional Facility that took the lives of forty-three inmates and guards in 1971, we have been made aware of the despair and rejection that prisoners often feel. They, too, demand that they be seen as persons and be given the basic rights due all human beings.

A few years ago, we began to focus on the women's liberation movement. Coretta King stated that she felt more discrimination as a woman than as a black person. Women's plea to be seen as persons of equal worth with men soon grew to the discovery that men also need to be freed from stereotypes. Human liberation suggests that all people need to be accepted as worthwhile human beings.

July 24

John 10:10b

Try an experiment today. Sit for an hour in a bus station or stand on the corner of a busy street. As the people pass by, think to yourself, "Each is a person, loved and valued by God"—the mother who slaps her children around, the dejected elderly couple, the street cleaner, the arrogant teenagers, the haughty matron.

Read your newspaper or watch your television with the thought in mind that every story is about a child of God—the boy who killed an elderly woman because he did not like old people, the power-hungry politician, the mayor and police chief charged with taking pay-offs from a gambler, the actress who pleaded to be seen as a person not as an alcoholic.

Everyone you have "met" today is a person of worth.

July 25

Luke 19:1-10

Peter was a fisherman—earthy, impulsive, hardly a likely candidate for top leadership in the kingdom. But Jesus saw in him a potential tower of strength. Zacchaeus was a tax collector and a cheat. The bystanders who saw Jesus enter his house could not understand why the Master would associate with a sinner. The scribes and Pharisees brought to Jesus a woman caught in adultery. The law demanded death by stoning but Jesus did not even condemn her. Her sin did not cancel the fact that she was a person of worth.

Jesus saw each person not for what he or she had been but for what he or she could become. The Samaritan woman at the well, the man with an unclean spirit, the rich young ruler, the little children—all were precious in his sight.

July 26

One of the beautiful messages of the New Testament is Jesus' acceptance of all persons, regardless of age, sex, nationality or station in life. However, one of the problems we face in seeing the worth of each person lies in our own self-image. In *No Longer Strangers* Bruce Larson suggests a revealing exercise. He tells us to list five of our liabilities, then five of our assets; and to time the number of minutes it takes to do each. What did this show us?

A popular book, *I'm OK, You're OK*, by Thomas A. Harris, claims that many people live their childhood with a "You're OK, but I'm not OK" attitude. In order to become whole persons this needs to change to "I'm OK, you're OK." Most of us need to affirm ourselves before we can grow to full ability to accept others.

July 27
John 13:34—35

Heavenly Father, help me know when I hear the preacher say everybody is your child, that includes me, too. In spite of all my failures and shortcomings, help me accept myself honestly as a person of worth. Give me a new vision of my possibilities and what I may become with your help. Then, God, open my eyes to appreciate the uniqueness and worth of each person I meet. May I somehow attain a degree of Jesus' ability to see the infinite possibilities in every individual. Free me from all forms of prejudice. I am sorry for sometimes being too judgmental and, at times, even snobbish. If I have rejected some who do not look like me or live my style of life, forgive me. Use me as an instrument for helping others to realize their worth. In Jesus' name. *Amen.*

Marilyn Taylor, Philadelphia, Pennsylvania

Salvation Today • July 28—August 3

SALVATION AND PERSONHOOD July 28

Most people *define* salvation from what they know of the Bible, but it is just as valid to *describe* it in relation to aspects of human experience. Salvation means coming to a right relationship with God—a sacrificial giving of ourselves to something higher than our possessions, our attitudes, and our life-styles. This is the stumbling block for modern-day Christians. As Jesus rightly understood, we are what we love and we become what we love. Salvation and the realization of personhood mean that we are free to open ourselves to the depth within our hearts which is the territory of God.

Lord, free us from the ties that bind the selfish heart, the narrowed mind. Open up our lives that we may live completed lives with thee. *Amen.*

Salvation and Justice
July 29

If we are to be saved fully in our lives as Christians, we need to become intimately involved with the moment of history in which we find ourselves. To do this, we must commit ourselves to the freedom and development of the lives of others. As long as injustice rules in the world, then we are never free to be saved alone. As God's children, we are held responsible to produce the conditions that will help make salvation possible to all. The individual who is open to salvation is not afraid of justice or of the changes it may bring but is made brave through faith in Christ and the love of Christ.

The Christ who frees the sinner's soul—who makes the shattered self a whole—is Christ to all, the poor, the weak. It's their salvation that we seek.

Salvation and Power
July 30

To be truly Christian and truly saved, we must consider the meaning and purpose of power. We need to understand that the power in the world that seems to be controlled by us comes ultimately from God. Power can be both creative and destructive, but the power to be saved means the ability to be humble, to assume responsibility, to be giving, and to understand the use and abuse of the power that is ours. We should neither fear, worship, nor manipulate power. The overwhelming power of our nation and our time must be approached with the desire to use its possibilities for human salvation rather than destruction.

Within our hands is life and death—the power to stifle human breath. Lord, help us have the clear insight to turn our power toward the right. *Amen.*

SALVATION AND REALITY — July 31

Very often our conception of salvation is unreal. We cannot comprehend the breadth and depth of the experience of God and of Jesus and so we create an unreal religion, filled with figures that are mythologized and popularized beyond recognition. We fail to see the miracle of God's presence in our own lives and in our own deep convictions. It is only when we approach our lives with realistic appraisal that we can be open to the power of salvation. Then we can see our faults as well as our strong points, and we are free to change and adapt to the real world and its experiences.

The mirror which reflects our lives reveals, Lord, how the Christian strives for understanding which must be illumined by the light of thee.

SALVATION AND FEAR — August 1

In our moments of fear we begin to shed the layers of the self with which we habitually clothe ourselves. We do not face ourselves completely until our existence is threatened. We fear death, we fear rejection, and we fear the emptiness of our days. The only way to deal with the overwhelming fears that fill our lives is to have confidence in the love of Christ which both protects and frees us. This is not to say that we can live completely without fear but we can come to see our fears in perspective. Christ came to free us from the self, from death, and from the fears that undo us.

The fears that make us mean and small and deaf to that much higher call will overwhelm us, Lord, if we cannot put all our trust in thee.

SALVATION AND SUFFERING   August 2

When we are at the edge of life, we can most appreciate the fullness of it. If we are able to face suffering and death, then we are free to love fully. Suffering is important because of what it helps us become. In suffering we can learn to see beyond ourselves and become open to the love of God. We take part in a truly universal human experience and also become one with our Lord since we, as Christians, have a God who suffers with us and for us. The new kingdom of Christ brought with it freedom from futility by giving a meaning to suffering and a promise of life after death.

Lord, in our suffering and our doubt, help us see the right way out—see the way beyond our tears to that which calms our hurts and fears. *Amen.*

SALVATION AND HOPE   August 3

Salvation opens the doors of the future. It does not dwell in the past and on tradition. If we are trapped in our traditions and our own concepts of religion, then there is no room for change and for new approaches to salvation. The hope that lies in salvation is that there is something more to live for than the limits of our own experience. Hope also means that salvation is free and freely given. The promise of a better life, a clearer understanding of ourselves, and a union with Christ is at the center of salvation.

The hope of that which is our being, beyond the limits of our seeing, beyond our own imagination, is the heart of our salvation.

Peggy Owen Clark, New York, New York

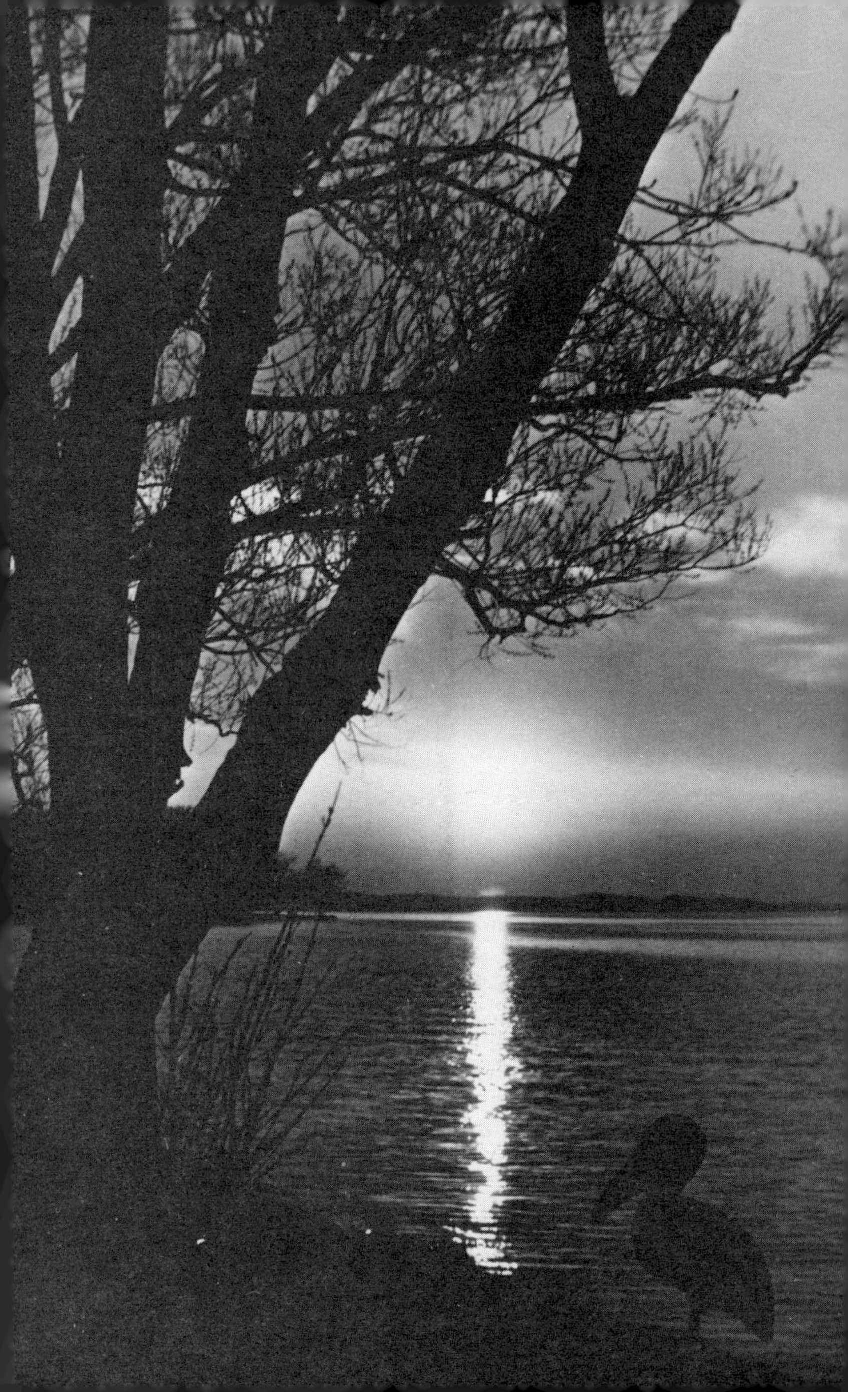

Bodies of Water I Have Known • August 4–10

August 4

Luke 13:29

The Florida Keys, leading to Key West, are a series of keys, or islands, connected by bridges. On one side of these barriers, the Atlantic Ocean flows past; on the other side, the Gulf of Mexico streams by.

Such is our world. Many barriers divide us, yet there are also meeting places—even as the ocean and the gulf come together under the bridges and finally merge at the foot of the Keys into one great body of water.

So today people and countries of our earth can come together to work out their problems. Christian love overcomes many obstacles.

The East and the West flow in separate currents but we all meet at the feet of our heavenly Father.

August 5

Jer. 16:18

Many years ago, as a young person in northern Ohio, I attended conference at Lakeside on Lake Erie. Our vespers were held each evening on the shore, where we could see the setting sun reflected in the lake. As the rays of light shone on the water, we could sense God's presence in the world. In recent years, I have read with sorrow of the pollution of this great lake by the industries along its shoreline. Our lives, too, become polluted by our actions and by the thoughts that accumulate over the years. But there is hope in spite of pollution. Even as the industries are cleaning up their discharges into Lake Erie, it is time for us to look seriously at ourselves and see how we can change our lives. Let us pray that they may ever more clearly reflect God's eternal love.

August 6

Recently my youngest daughter and I were walking along the beach near our home when she found a sand dollar. Shaped like a silver dollar, this unusual shell found in the Gulf of Mexico comes in many sizes.

There is a legend that these shells symbolize the birth, life, and death of Christ. Five holes pierce the shell, representing the nail holes in the hands and feet of Christ and the wound in his side made by a Roman spear. On one face of the sand dollar is the shape of an Easter lily and on the reverse side the Christmas poinsettia appears. Inside the shell are five white doves, representing our hopes for goodwill and peace on earth. This legend of a simple seashell helps us tell in a wonderful way the story of Christ's life.

August 7

"Thy word is a lamp to my feet
 and a light to my path" (Psalm 119:105, RSV).

Beyond the sand dunes at the northern edge of Lake Michigan, is a lighthouse known as Point Betsie. Its light shines far out across the lake, warning passing ships to avoid this point of land; it is also a landmark, so that the ships will know their location.

Our Bible warns us of many dangers and pitfalls. Yet, when we are seeking our way in this world, it is a beacon to guide us to safety. If we will let God guide us as surely as the lighthouse beacon guides passing ships, we may become a reflection of his light for others.

Father, may we so reflect your light in our lives that others may come to know you. *Amen.*

August 8
Col. 3:13—14

There are many lakes in northern Michigan, but Lakes Cadillac and Mitchell are unusual in that they are connected by a canal. Strangely, in the winter months when both lakes are frozen to a depth of at least forty inches, the water in the canal remains free-flowing.

Sometimes when we have had a disagreement with a friend and cannot find a way to bridge this trouble, we need to remember that God's love is like a canal between us—always free-flowing and open.

As we come to God in prayer, let us open our lives and become immersed in this great love flowing from him. We will find that his love flowing in us can heal our broken relationships, overcoming even a bitter quarrel or disagreement.

August 9

"Keep your heart with all vigilance;
　for from it flow the springs of life" (Prov. 4:23, RSV).

In Florida, springs are used for many purposes such as swimming and scuba diving. These springs gush from underground in torrents of clear, cold water. Those who dive in them say the light deep within is beautiful because of the purity of the water.

In this verse of Proverbs is a guide for all Christians. If we keep our hearts pure and clean, then our lives, too, will be beautiful. It is not easy to keep our hearts pure in today's world but as Christians we should try to show God's love in the lives we lead. As the springs of water flow in purity from the heart of the earth, so may the love of our Savior ever flow from our hearts to others.

August 10
Rev. 22:1

From a hillside in northern Michigan can be seen a view of the various depths of the water in Crystal Lake. Nearest the shoreline the water is a grayish-blue. As the lake deepens, the color changes until, close to the center, it is a deep, deep blue and crystal clear.

When we first begin to respond to Christ, our lives are a little indefinite like the grayish-blue color of the shallow water. We have not yet waded into the depths that are waiting for us. These changing colors are like our lives. As we surrender more of ourselves to God's will, our lives become truer and deeper. When we commit ourselves totally to God's will, we find our purpose in life.

God, grant us the ability to see your will in our lives. *Amen.*

Georgia Meece, Sarasota, Florida

Practicing the Presence of God • August 11–17

SEEK THE LORD

August 11
1 Chron. 16:8–12

"Seek the Lord and his strength,
seek his presence continually!" (1 Chron. 16:11, RSV.)

There are times in the life of each of us when we need a greater strength than our own, a deeper love, a more profound faith, a more steadfast hope with which to face the stress of everyday living. We know that, if we could open our lives to God, we would receive help, but with Job we cry out, "Oh, that I knew where I might find him" (Job 23:3a, RSV). Only in prayer do we meet our God face to face, knowing that he is a loving and all-wise Father yearning for us to come to him in trust that he might give direction to our life.

O God, above all else we would know thee. Take our trembling hands in thine and draw us into thy presence. *Amen.*

The Quietness of God

August 12
Psalm 46

"Be still, and know that I am God" (Psalm 46:10a, RSV).

In our hurried and harried lives we seldom find the time to be still. Yet, it is necessary for us to cultivate a quiet time each day when we can be alone with God and feel his healing and peace. It makes a marked difference in our day if, in the quietness of the morning, we read God's word with an expectant heart, voice a prayer of thanksgiving for his care, and seek direction for our activities. An extended opportunity will come at night—a time for reviewing our day; thanking God for his presence; asking for his forgiveness; and committing ourselves, our loved ones, and our concerns into his keeping.

Father, in the stillness we seek thee. Fill us with thy presence. Bring us into quiet harmony with thy will. *Amen.*

The Joy of Thanksgiving

August 13
Psalm 100

"Enter his gates with thanksgiving,
 and his courts with praise!" (Psalm 100:4a, RSV.)

Singing God's praises should be as natural as breathing for those who have an awareness of the goodness of God. We name our blessings—not on,y the material ones but also those of the spirit. We thank God for the privilege of prayer, for love, understanding, and faith. We thank him for the gift of his Son, Jesus Christ, and for what he means to us. Also we thank God for each obstacle in our path, for it is through overcoming our troubles with God's help that our faith is strengthened. True blessings and the presence of God are known only to the grateful.

We give thanks, O God, and sing thy praises. *Amen.*

IF WE CONFESS OUR SINS — August 14
Luke 18:9–14

"God, be merciful to me a sinner!" (Luke 18:13b, RSV.)

As we thank God for his goodness and mercy to us, we become painfully aware of our unworthiness. Our mask is dropped and all pretense gone. God knows our sins and so do we, so we can be specific about them, confessing those things that are not in accordance with his will. Only in prayer can we open ourselves to God, knowing he is a loving father who will forgive us, help us correct our mistakes, and give us another chance to fulfill his purpose for us. In accepting his forgiveness and surrendering our will to his we are restored to fellowship with him.

Give us, our Father, the courage to open our hearts to thee, the willingness to accept thy forgiveness and the strength to walk in newness of life. *Amen.*

PROMISE OF GOD — August 15
1 John 3:18–24

". . . and we receive from him whatever we ask, because we keep his commandments and do what pleases him" (1 John 3:22, RSV).

This is, indeed, a wonderful promise. We are invited to take to God all our cares and concerns for ourselves and others. All he asks is that we believe in his Son, Jesus Christ, keep his commandments, and open our hearts to his guidance. All our petitions will be answered according to our needs. God's ways are not our ways, and his answer may not be what we expected. To know his guidance we must be sensitive to his voice as he speaks to us through Jesus Christ, the Bible, the universe, persons of great faith, and the action of the Holy Spirit.

Loving Father, tune our ears to hear thy voice. *Amen.*

THY WILL BE DONE   August 16
                                       Luke 22:39—44

". . . not my will, but thine, be done" (Luke 22:42b, RSV).

In time of great need, Jesus prayed that not his will but his Father's might be done. When we pray in this way, submitting our will to the divine will, we relinquish our problems and needs into God's keeping and with perfect faith we trust him. We cannot bend God's will to our will. Our trust in him is never misplaced. Although his answer to our petition may be No, we have the assurance of his love and that what he wills for us will be best, in accordance with his wisdom and purpose for our life.

Dear Father, give us the grace to trust thee more and to accept willingly thy will for our life. *Amen.*

POWER OF THE HOLY SPIRIT   August 17
                                       1 John 4:13—21

"By this we know that we abide in him and he in us, because he has given us of his own Spirit" (1 John 4:13, RSV).

The great Japanese Christian Kagawa said that prayer is not effectual until we rise from our knees with a tool in our hands, dedicated and ready for service. Real prayer leads to action. It deepens our concern and leads us to accept responsibility to help those for whom we pray. If in our prayer we commit ourselves to his purpose, God will manifest his power through us and we will become instruments in his hands to serve others.

O God, may I live each day with the assurance of thy presence. Grant that my life may become the dwelling place of thy Holy Spirit that I may do thy will. *Amen.*

Louise Pratt, Shreveport, Louisiana

Road Signs of Life • August 18−24

FOUR WAY STOP　　　　　　　　　　　　August 18

Have you ever come to a four-way stop while driving, only to find that one, two, or three other drivers all got there at the same time? Life is like that. We come to a deadlock in decision-making at work or at church, or we come to a stand-off in personal relationships. That is when someone has to take a risk and make the first move or have the patience to see someone else go ahead.

Either way takes courage, and a Christian attitude takes patience, unselfishness and clear thinking. The person who thinks only of herself—of getting started on her way again or getting her idea across—can often end up hurting someone else as well as herself. This stop is a time for caution, whether driving or living. Only with love, courtesy, and concern can we break the four-way stops.

REST AREA AHEAD　　　　　　　　　　　August 19

It was a hot summer day in Texas. A traveling family had stopped along the road to eat lunch under the scorching sun. They did not know that just around the big bend in the road ahead of them was a beautiful, shady roadside rest area with tables, benches, water, and other conveniences. Texas highways are dotted with such rest areas, but they are not always available at the right time.

We don't have to travel life's road waiting for a rest area. Christ's promise, "Come unto me all ye that labour and are heavy laden, and I will give you rest" (Matt. 11:28, KJV), is available to us at all times. All we have to do is lean on him now and shift our burdens to him. We don't have to wait for a rest area to appear. Christ will lift our load and see us through.

YIELD   August 20

She was an elderly resident at Juliette Fowler Homes in Dallas. I had visited with her a number of times before but now she told me she had lost her sight. When I expressed my sorrow and concern, she interrupted me. "Oh, no," she said, as her face lit up with a glow of excitement and anticipation, "don't feel that way. Just think, the next thing I see will be my Master's face."

Life can be beautiful when we know how and when to yield. When we see circumstances of life that we cannot change, it takes courage to accept them gracefully and "in every thing give thanks" (1 Thess. 5:18a, KJV). Though blind, this friend could see beyond her handicap to a bright tomorrow. Like Paul, she knew how to yield herself to God's way.

SLOW   August 21

We do not like to go slowly. The faster we can travel, the better we like it. Our calendars are jammed. Our lives are like Kleenex boxes, with one event popping up after another. *Slow* signs at school zones, street repair areas and dangerous intersections irritate us. But we need to slow down the machinery of our lives.

We need to quiet our minds—to be still and know that God is. Jesus withdrew from the throngs to be with his Father in meditation and prayer. We need to fill our lives with quietness and let prayer spread throughout our daily occupations. Let us be thankful for the *Slow* signs in our lives—waiting at a red light, for a doctor's appointment, for children to come out of school. We can use these moments to draw near to God and he will draw near to us.

U TURN   August 22

Did you ever get on the wrong road and not be able to find a place to turn around? To see a U Turn sign and know you can get back on the right track is indeed a welcome sight. Christ is constantly offering us a place to turn around and follow him. No matter how far we might go in the wrong direction, we can always make a U Turn and get back with Christ.

The decision is ours. You and I must do the turning. It is comforting to know that God never turns, never changes. He is always the same and always available. A favorite hymn points out that his faithfulness is great, that there is no shadow of turning with him. By following Christ, we can be sure that we are going in the right direction for he leads us into paths of righteousness.

DETOUR   August 23

Detours are annoying. It's often unpleasant to leave the main highway and travel over an unknown road that usually isn't as good as the one it is replacing. We don't like detours in daily life, either. We have goals and objectives toward which we are working and to get off the direct path to what we want is disturbing.

Detours usually are for our own good, however. They steer us around pitfalls, smooth out rough spots or take out a dangerous curve. Usually on a detour we cannot see what we would have met on the main road but we have to trust the highway engineers. For the Christian, the road of life is similar. We can't see how much better the detours are for us. We just need to remember that if in all our ways we acknowledge God, he will direct our path.

Two-Way Traffic   August 24

Many times in driving we prefer one-way traffic, but our relationship with God is always two-way, if we desire it. God reaches out to us in his love and saving grace and we respond in acceptance and thanksgiving. This is the beautiful, two-way relationship that God desires with all his children.

The only time this relationship is one-way is when we fail to respond to him, rejecting him and his love. Even then he is still reaching out to us, seeking us in every way he can, waiting patiently for our acceptance. Such a one-way relationship can be very lonely. As on a one-way street, we never see anyone else face to face. Thank God for two-way traffic with him.

Virginia Dixon, Dallas, Texas

Grace • August 25−31

Pass It On   August 25

John 14:12−13; Matt. 5:46

Jesus touched the leper, the blind, the sinner. He told us that we would do greater things than he because he would be with us always. He passed his love on to us. Grace is this undeserved love that we must pass on to others.

We are asked to love the unlovely. It was easy to embrace sweet little Amy but Joe was a wretched troublemaker. Yet he was transformed when he was impulsively hugged and asked, "Joe, how can we help you?" His crossed eyes shone with the newness of an acceptance he had never known before. As a teacher, I see the unlovely often as the discipline problems of the class and of the world. They need acceptance if they are to change. We have been accepted and loved; this grace must be passed on.

God, thank you for accepting and using even us. *Amen.*

A NEIGHBOR   August 26
                                          1 John 4:7—21

We've been blessed with a neighbor who was never too busy to share our trials and triumphs of daily living. She anticipated our need for friendship or for privacy, for a spare guest room, a helping hand, a listening ear, a babysitter, or just reassurance. We felt secure knowing she prayed for us daily. She was a gift from God. If you have ever known such love, you've known grace.

If we can be that kind of neighbor, we have really understood what Christ meant when he told us to love our neighbor as ourself. The world would be a lonely place without such unselfish love. My neighbor was never alone for she was at one with God. This difference is the secret of my neighbor's grace. "If we love one another, God lives in us" (1 John 4:12b, TEV).

GRACE OF A THORN   August 27
                                           2 Cor. 12:7—10

A once active, carefree girl was strung up in traction—forced to call on power greater than her own and to submit all the corners of her independence in total obedience to God. She prayed, "Heal me if that is your will but I accept this pain and even the possibility of being an invalid. Your will be done." New heights are reached from new depths endured. A well-known hymn came alive for me as I *walked* to a hospital chapel that day. The unexplained love through healing is truly *amazing grace*. A life so touched by the Creator still has its thorns but I'm grateful for these, "for when I am weak, then I am strong" (2 Cor. 12:10b, TEV).

When I was submissive, God changed my days.
I learned grace isn't earned. Doxology's my praise!

THE GIFT OF TIME   August 28
                                          Eccl. 3:1−13

How does a Christian use his gift of time? Jesus gave no possessions to people but he gave his time. He gave himself to children, to the disciples, to the lame, to his enemies. As a minister's wife, I realize that great works cannot be done by clergy alone. One man can't equal a congregational army, serving with all their talent, time, and money. In our congregation, we've seen people invest themselves in the ministry of building a church. In this stewardship we've reaped dividends of fellowship, vitality, and trust, as well as new, debt-free structures.

> Live each moment as if it were your last;
> Remember everything you do creates your past.
> If you seek God's will and give him the glory,
> Life will unfold a wonderful story.

GRACE FOR A MOTHER   August 29
                                          Psalm 139:23−24

What do we parents give of the life we live?
Talent, work, love, faith in God above.
However hectic, these are the best days of life.
Looking back you see no strife
But love in the dirty little face—
Unselfish valentine in torn lace.
Walls have the treasured art of handprints,
Even furniture reads memories etched in dents.
God, give me the grace of a listening ear,
Sympathetic wisdom to quiet a fear,
A little time to read and think alone,
Strength when I'm tired to the bone.
Father, as a child of God, teach me
    A Christian mother to be. *Amen.*

IT'S MY WORLD　　　　　　　　　　　August 30

Gen. 1:26−31

"It is good . . ." At sunrise the world seemed new.
　　The tides erased footprints and litter, too.
　　Only the "Danger" sign remains each morning,
　　Giving people walking the sand bar a warning.
"It is good . . ." The crabs were plentiful that day.
　　A mother bird showed her babies the way
　　To pick and eat on the run
　　When a spaniel chased them for fun.
　　Then Mrs. Bird fluttered but couldn't fly away.
　　Around in a circle, then on the sand she lay.
　　The surprised cocker gave her curious sniffs,
　　While his owner the sick seabird lifts.
"It was good . . ." But the world grows old and badly used.
"Danger! Water Poison!" A sign for birds we've abused.

THE GIFT OF HEARING　　　　　　　　August 31

Isa. 50:4−5

What would have happened if others had failed to listen as we often do? Moses would have doused the burning bush. Noah might have said, "Sorry, God, I get seasick." Saul might have said, "You can't change me, God. I *know* I ought to persecute Christians." The disciples might have protested, "We aren't qualified; get someone else, Jesus." But these people did listen. Do we hear God through the silent cries all about us? Do we listen in our families, schools, the world? A small child is mute because no one speaks with her. An elderly woman wrote on every page of her diary, "No one came today." Runaway youth experiment with freedom, sex, drugs and find only despair. Many live without Christ—no one to care. Let us listen to God. Let us listen to others. Grace to hear is a gift. Listen!
. . .

Elaine G. Adams, Athens, Georgia

Love • September 1–7

WHAT IS LOVE? September 1

1 John 4:7–21

Love is the one part of life that most occupies and controls our thoughts, our emotions, our very being. It becomes real to each of us in a different way. Some find it in a close one-to-one relationship with God. Most find love, however, through those who live God's love on earth, who allow God to reveal his love through them, even as Christ revealed God's love to us. We sing, "They'll know we are Christians by our love!" But daily we find giving love is extremely complex. We need patience and caring about every feeling, thought, and need of those we love. Our actions, not just our words, let others know.

What are the attributes of God's love? Delicacy, intricacy, mystery, limitless capacity, ingenuity, completeness. God is Love. *Do I let his love show in my life?*

THE DELICACY OF LOVE September 2

1 John 4:18

Love's delicacy is like a butterfly's wings—
> withstanding many a buffeting wind and storm;
> blown off course, perhaps, but ever seeking
> to return; strengthened in unseen power.

The butterfly appears fragile, yet it survives unbelievable buffeting. Hurt is inevitable. God, the unseen power, can bring us back on course. Strength can come, healing can come, no matter how battered we may be—if we can accept it. God's power, expressed in the lives of others, can help us accept ourselves in all our delicacy and weakness as well as in our strength. *When I hurt someone, can I seek forgiveness? When I am hurt, can I accept healing love? Do I really believe love is stronger than hate?*

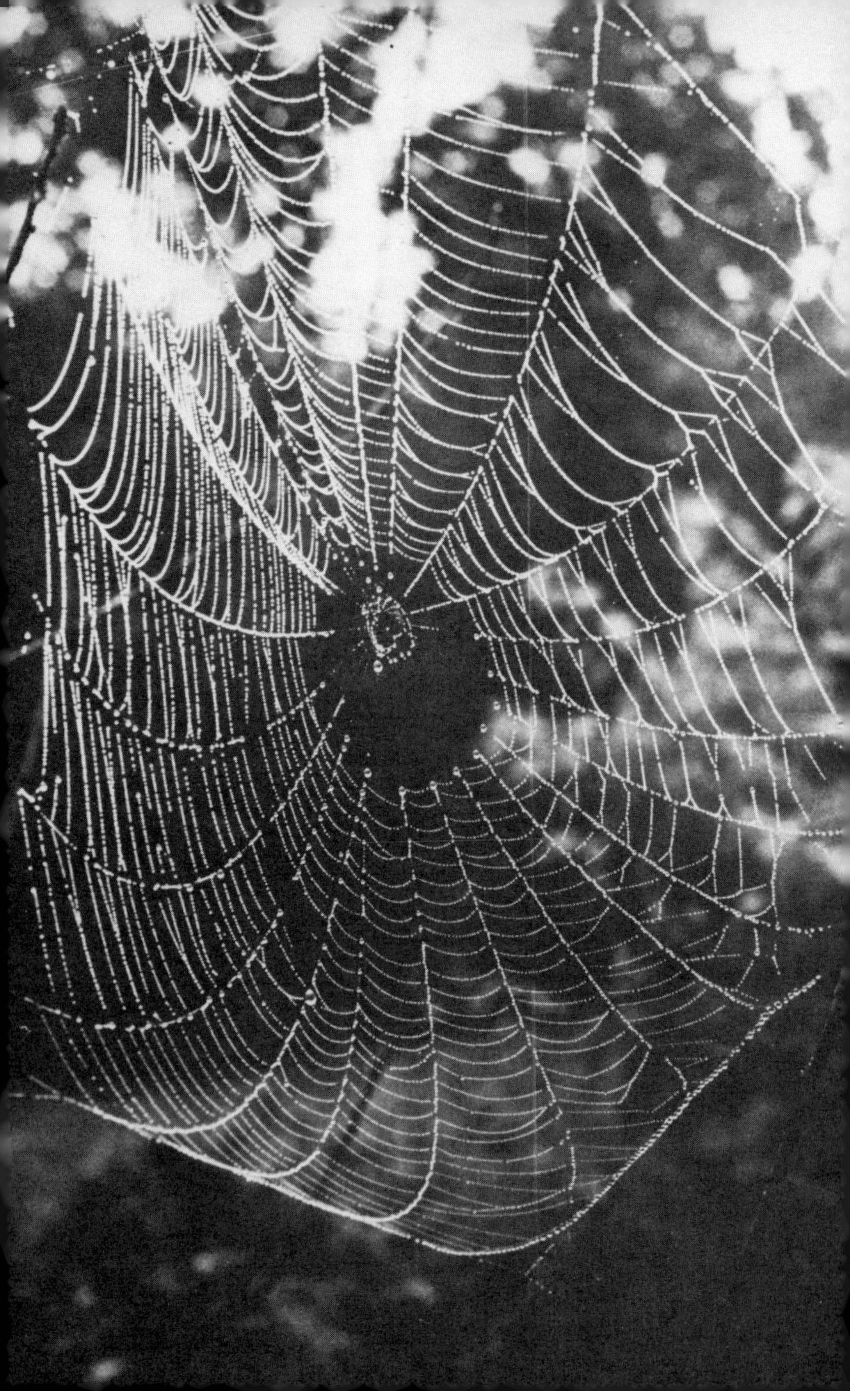

THE INTRICACY OF LOVE   September 3

Love's intricacy is like a spider's web—
> woven and interwoven; holding fast, sticking tightly; spanning unexpected distances; appearing at unexpected places; patiently respinnable.

A spider's web in early morning dew has unbelievable intricacy of pattern. It shows the unlimited patience of repeated spinning efforts. We find it in most unexpected places. So it is with God's love. Unexpectedly we feel the touch of one who cares. In deep anguish, strength comes from an unexpected source. We try and try, are tempted to give up—yet God holds on through those who love us. *When I feel broken and shattered, do I care enough about myself to seek a way to respin the web of my life, to find the beauty of God's pattern for me?*

THE MYSTERY OF LOVE   September 4

Love's mystery is like the far-reaching heavens—
> wondered about; questioned; bit by bit more understood; requiring unbelievable daring, courage, and risk to reach to its unknown depths.

Love is a mystery. We can't know about it, we can only slowly learn to comprehend its depths and intensity. Even when we feel we have all knowledge, we need faith to reach into the unknown. We reach out for love in faith. We accept one another in faith. We have no guarantee, only wonder at God's great love, forgiveness, and acceptance, expressed in those who love, forgive, and accept us. *Is it any wonder I don't always understand others when so often I don't understand even myself? Can I risk loving another first, rather than waiting for someone to love me?*

THE CAPACITY OF LOVE   September 5
                              1 Cor. 13

Love's capacity is like the ocean—
> immeasurable; limitless; impossible to see all at one time; constantly resurging, renewing, refilling; overwhelmingly changeable.

Love's capacity is boundless. The more we give away, the more we have to give. As love divides, it multiplies. Hold tightly to a handful of sand, it slips away. Open your hand, it remains full and heaped up. So it is with love. We have unlimited capacity for love—but we must be open to receive it. We have immeasurable capacity for pain, too, often having to live with limitations and accept what cannot be changed. When we give up, God sends someone to tie a knot in our rope of life so we can hang on. *Have I patience to wait for the renewal of love's incoming tide?*

THE INGENUITY OF LOVE   September 6
                              2 Tim. 1:7

Love's ingenuity is like the body—
> thinking, analyzing, planning; acting creatively, giving, taking; feeling, hurting; accepting, forgiving, trusting, healing.

Love is ingenious—not all logic, not all feeling but a blending of the two. Our whole life follows a pattern of crucifixion and resurrection but we must deeply experience God's love in some relationship before we can accept crucifixion. Crucifixion comes before resurrection; pain before joy; trust before healing; healing before peace. Whatever we've been, God accepts and forgives if we are willing. Whatever we've been, one who loves us accepts and forgives if we are willing. *Is someone waiting for me to say, "I love you as you are!" Am I willing?*

THE ENTIRETY OF LOVE	September 7

Love's entirety is like the Spirit of God—
patient, boundless; unboxable, indefinable; unsurpassable; soul-shaping; flaming; free; eternal.

God's Spirit cannot be boxed. Nor can our love for one another be limited, except by us. We accept love's delicacy and intricacy in the lives of those we touch. We seek to discover the mystery and capacity of God's love. We try to allow love's ingenuity to make us creative and giving, to help us trust, be healed, accept what cannot be changed, live above our limitations.

Melt us with your strength, God. Mold us with your ingenious power. Fill us with your Spirit. Use us. Help us love freely as you love. Lead us to life eternal. *Amen.*

Lois Jean Pew, Chico, California

A Life of Service • September 8—14

TOWARD A BETTER WORLD	September 8

Rom. 5:1—5

What can I do to help make this a better world? As I see it, I am in a whole world of new ideas and new courses of action. For a meaningful existence, I must learn to accept the changes for good and work to help solve the difficult problems that are confronting me. There are great things to be done and God expects me to help. I receive his boundless love; then I must share it with others. Hands reach out to me for friendship and my hands can be used in service for God. I can teach and share my understanding and love with others. I can have a more abundant life if I serve as a personal witness in new ways.

Dear God, I thank you for the many opportunities for service. *Amen.*

CHRISTIAN RESPONSE September 9

1 Cor. 13

Forty-seven years in the classroom of public schools, with twenty years of that time devoted to meeting the individual needs of educable, mentally retarded children, have given me an understanding of what it means for anyone to be underprivileged. When I was called to serve the retarded, I felt unworthy. In gratitude for God's goodness to me I accepted, and prayerfully each day I dedicated myself to this work. Never for a moment was it easy. But it was always joyous. The devotion and loyalty of those children are still with me, as I continue my work with private pupils. My retirement from the public school is only a challenge for service in new ways.

God, help us to recognize new challenges for service and to accept them in thy name. *Amen.*

RENEWING YOUR SPIRIT September 10

Psalm 25:1–12

Modern living makes extensive, exacting demands upon children as well as adults. Out of this chaos, we recognize more emotionally disturbed children and more adults with no purpose in life. It is true we are living in stirring, insecure, and soul-searching days but haste and worry and expecting too much of each other will only add to our problems. Let us slow down and keep our lives in balance. Let us begin each day by thanking God for all our blessings. Let us take time for meditation through prayer and reading the Scriptures. Let us learn to be quiet and spend some time alone with God. He will strengthen us and prepare us for further service in a world that is so much in need of us.

Dear Lord, help us to be still and know that you are God and that you can direct our lives. *Amen.*

IN TIMES LIKE THESE   September 11
                             Matt. 13:31−32

So many massive scientific and political forces are at work in the world today that an individual can feel quite helpless. One could say that there is nothing one person can do. But if our lives are a source of light, and millions of other persons produce even a spark each, then the glow can become a fantastic radiance that will bring warmer, brighter relationships throughout the world. As Christians, our lives can become significant when we join other Christians in producing friendship among the nations of the earth. This is a wonderful way to help God's kingdom grow among us. If we let God rule our hearts we will learn how to help in times like these.

Heavenly Father, show us how we can help your kingdom grow. *Amen.*

WORKING HUMBLY   September 12
                            Eph. 6:1−8

There are many ways of working for Jesus. Christian service is not confined to church-related activities. We can also glorify God by faithfully executing our tasks wherever we may be. As Christians, we can go about our duties without worrying and grumbling. If we work at our tasks joyfully and prayerfully, our reward is inner happiness while our spirit becomes contagious for others around us. The plainest, everyday performances begin to take on a new look and can be accomplished with greater ease when we serve with a Christian attitude. It is only by God's grace and love that we are able to serve him.

O Lord, make my spirit such that I may ever walk humbly with you. *Amen.*

COMMUNITY SERVICE September 13
Luke 10:29—37

At times in our personal struggles we may become sorry for ourselves. This will never happen if we but look around us for places where we can put Christian ideas into action. Volunteer services are always needed in organized groups such as the Red Cross, associations for retarded and physically handicapped, day care centers, senior citizen groups, hospital auxiliaries, nursing homes for the aged, and youth groups. Indifference to the needs of others can breed only selfishness within us. Let us forget ourselves and get into action for there is no greater reward than knowing we have helped relieve the burdens of others. Through service we can experience love.

Thank you, God, for our brothers and sisters, with whom we may share your love. *Amen.*

WHERE IS YOUR FAITH? September 14
1 John 5:4—5

Are we seeking to know and do God's will or are we too busy with material things? Why are we fearful that we cannot overcome the frustrations of each day? Perhaps we have misplaced our values or have taken everything in our own hands. Naturally all has gone wrong if we have forgotten to ask God's guidance. Let us put our trust in him and he will give us courage and understanding. If we try to keep up with the frantic pace of life, rather than trying to follow the will of God, we are not serving him truly. Instead of looking elsewhere for help, let us remember to rely on God to help us overcome all obstacles.

Dear God, help us remember that you are our refuge and strength. Help us call upon you in faith. *Amen.*

Bertha Westbrook, Dunn, North Carolina

Two Minutes to God • September 15-21

BIT OF HEAVEN	September 15

Matt. 7:1-2, 8; 11:29. Rom. 12:2, 17-21

Neither pressure for time, nor poky children, nor cranky husband, nor balky appliances, nor noise, nor heat, nor pain shall dim the witness of God's Holy Spirit shining through me.

If the minor irritations of life upset us, let us learn to see beyond. Let us see our child, or husband, or the faulty situation as each should be. We can help anyone become the wonderful person God intended by accepting, expecting, and picturing each one as if he already were so—and he will be!

Each of us—mother, wife, teacher, secretary, grandmother—is the key. If we can keep ourselves a center of peace and love, situations near us will reflect this spirit. If we set the stage for God's kingdom on earth by living in Christ, a bit of God's heaven will surround us.

DARE TO PRAY	September 16

Matt. 17:20; 18:19-20; 21:21-22

One second is time for a prayer thought. In two minutes—in traffic, before church, waiting for the bus—spend one minute getting your mind off yourself. "O Lord, silence my five senses that I may hear inwardly." Consciously create a vacuum. In the second minute—ask God to fill you top to toe with his Holy Spirit. Do you dare spend two hours, or two days, or two weeks in communion with your Lord? If you do, you will be a changed person, a blessing to those around you.

Pray when you go to the door or answer the phone—when you're angry, when you're happy. God is a constant source of power, always ready to counsel and guide. After death perhaps we will understand more about the tremendous power of prayer and regret using it so little.

THE MIRACLE OF YOU — September 17
Gen. 1:27–28. Eph. 3:13–19

Think of a tiny, perfect grain of sand under a magnifying glass—and then think of a vast desert. Think of looking through a microscope at a single drop of water—and then of the mighty, billowing oceans. Think of our tiny earth—and the magnitude of the galaxies. Have you looked down into the Grand Canyon—or up at Mt. Hood? Have you thought of the millions of microscopic creatures in your own backyard—and of the tremendous variety of plants and animals in the oceans and on the continents? Have you ever felt unloved, unwanted, lonely, worthless, utterly insignificant—and then realized again the power, might, and glory beyond imagination of Almighty God?

God created *you* in his own image. *You* are a child of God.

ACT, DON'T REACT — September 18
Matt. 7:12. Gal. 5:1; 6:1–2

Confrontations bombard us in our world today. The secret of meeting these is to act—not react. To be like Christ, we must see through Christ's eyes, hear through his ears and pattern our thoughts, words, and actions after his. We have little or no control over the external factors of our lives—where we are born, who our parents are, the color of our skin. But we *are* the rulers of our thoughts, our words, and our actions. For our soul's health, we must seek not honor, worldly riches, transitory pleasures—but a clear conscience, a life in Christ, and joy everlasting.

Father, help us so to condition our hearts that we will follow your holy teachings. Grant that they may sink into our souls like dew into the grass until they permeate every aspect of our living. *Amen.*

WHATSOEVER   September 19
                                        Matt. 6:13. Phil. 4:8−9

Christ said in the Sermon on the Mount that the pure in heart are blessed. But how can we keep our minds—and even more important, our children's minds—pure in the midst of all the obscenity that is permitted in society today? My mother did it with the *whatsoevers*—whatever is true, honest, just, pure, lovely, of good report, think about these. She taught us when anything evil came into our minds to push it out by thinking of something good—to hold in our thoughts only the good, the true, and the beautiful.

Father, teach us what is acceptable and pleasing to you. And help us teach others, by our example, to withdraw from anything that leads to wrong but to work for virtues that we need. Help us see and avoid and fight evil but to see and follow good examples in others. *Amen.*

DO WE BELIEVE?   September 20
                                        Matt. 25:31−46; 28:18−20

If we really believed that those who do not minister to the hungry, the stranger, the sick, or the prisoner will "go away into eternal punishment" (Matt. 25:46a, RSV), we would work without ceasing to reach through our life and through our giving those who need our loving care.

There are some people whose lives our life does not touch. We reach them by sending the Good News through our outreach giving. There are some people whose lives are so closely related to ours that whatever affects us affects them. Here is our most difficult missionary job. They hear not what we say but what we do. If we really believed God's Word, we would really work to reach those who suffer. God loves us so much he sent his only Son, who commissioned us to preach, baptize, and teach his way of love.

ON FIRE
September 21

John 3:16

What does it *take* to get us excited? As channels of the good news of salvation through Christ, we ought to be on fire, bubbling over with enthusiasm and joy as we tell what Christ means to us. But how do we maintain this exuberance? The Christian way is a three-act play.

First, we receive God's great love just as we are—imperfect, impure, unlovely but forgiven, accepted, and loved. Second, we accept ourselves; if God loves, forgives, and wants us; we must love ourselves. Third, we then reach out with concern, respect, understanding, and love to other people. God loves us because of—and in spite of—what we are; we, in turn, love and serve others.

Jeanne Rush, Roland, Arkansas

The Fruit of the Spirit • September 22–28

LOVE
September 22

Gal. 5:22–23; Heb. 12:6a

Love has many faces, but each one involves discipline. Recently my four-year-old granddaughter, in a fit of anger, ransacked her room. Since she was not punished, she decided to do a repeat the next night when I was babysitting. I sternly reminded her that I would not tolerate such naughtiness. She was made to pick up everything she had pulled down, take her bath, and go to bed. As I lifted her out of the bathtub and sat her on a towel in my lap, she threw her arms around my neck and said, "Dinny, I love you better than anyone in the whole world but we mustn't tell anyone; they wouldn't understand." Because of the love that has always existed between us, she knew I disciplined her from love. So it is with God's love. He tempers and prunes for service and growth.

JOY AND PEACE	September 23

Psalm 51:12

One usually thinks of joy in connection with exhilaration and hilarity but there is a deeper sense of joy that carries with it peace. A few days ago, I stood with a friend who had watched her mother suffer through a long illness. When the end came, instead of being overcome with grief, my friend seemed to feel a deep peace, even joy, in the knowledge that her mother had been released from pain and had gone to a place with God for which she had prepared herself. To a Christian, death should be a time of rejoicing, remembering Jesus' words, "I go to prepare a place for you . . . I will come again and will take you to myself" (John 14:2b—3a, RSV).

Dear God, may we come to know thy joy and peace which passes understanding. *Amen.*

PATIENCE (LONG-SUFFERING)	September 24

Gal. 6:9

Recently, as I walked through the park with my two beautiful, healthy granddaughters, we saw a mother patiently working with her young son. His legs were encased in braces. Perspiration poured from the faces of both from the physical strain of trying to take just a few steps. When the effort finally bore fruit, there was joy and praise from the proud parent.

The three of us learned a lesson of loving patience that day that I'm sure we will never forget.

Jesus never once told his disciples that following him would be easy.

Our heavenly Father, help us learn that those who "wait upon the LORD shall renew their strength" (Isa. 40:31, KJV). *Amen.*

GENTLENESS AND GOODNESS — September 25
Isa. 53:7b

In our age of humanism, any show of gentleness or goodness may be considered weakness. We put great stress on physical prowess and demonstrations of strength, both as individuals and as nations. Often the one who puts up the greatest bluff is the biggest coward.

From our study of the Bible we know Jesus was capable of showing great physical and moral courage, as when he thought his Father's house was being desecrated.

It must have taken great physical and emotional stamina to walk the countryside, teaching, healing, and preaching day after day; but Jesus came to show the true nature of God, a part of which is gentleness and goodness.

As we strive to be more like Jesus, may we learn to emulate him in gentleness and goodness.

FAITH — September 26
John 20:29b

One night, after I had put my four-year-old granddaughter to bed, she called to me, "Dinny, I wish you would come to bed. I'm afraid." I reminded her that her older sister was asleep in the next bed, that I was just across the hall, and besides God was there with her. Her answer jarred me because it spoke volumes about our faith when she said, "Yes, but I want somebody with skin on that I can see. He can't talk."

That is exactly what Jesus had in mind when he said to Thomas, "Because thou hast seen me, thou hast believed . . ." (John 20:29a, KJV). We, as Christians, must walk by faith and not by sight because we see many things "through a glass, darkly; but then face to face" (1 Cor. 13:12a, KJV).

Father, we do believe. Help our unbelief. *Amen.*

HUMILITY (MEEKNESS)　　　　　　　September 27
　　　　　　　　　　　　　　　　　Mark 9:35b

The story is told of the late great Christian citizen, George Washington Carver, that once he was called to Washington to receive the President's citation for his contribution to his country and fellowmen. He slipped off the train in his rumpled clothes, with battered suitcase, and melted away in the crowd while celebrities and newsmen waited for the great scientist to disembark. Such humility is indeed rare in an age when people are prone to glorify self and rise often on the shoulders of their fellows.

Jesus, repeatedly spoken of as the suffering servant, often reminded his hearers that he did nothing of himself but only through the will and purpose of his Father.

Dear Father, help us lose ourselves in loving service to thee and to others. *Amen.*

SELF-CONTROL (TEMPERANCE)　　　　September 28
　　　　　　　　　　　　　　　　　1 Tim. 4:12b

One of the hardest things to acquire in life is temperance or self-control. David was aware of this when he cried out, "Create in me a clean heart, O God; and renew a right spirit within me" (Psalm 51:10, KJV).

Like David, we should be ever mindful of the need for the Holy Spirit in our lives to renew, discipline, and create. We are so frail and human that alone we are simply incapable of self-control. Each has her own special shortcoming that needs attention. Often it is the tongue!

Jesus has said, "I will not leave you desolate; I will come to you" (John 14:18, RSV). Let us claim that promise each day for help in self-control.

Lord, mold me, fill me, use me. *Amen.*

Gladys H. Meisburg, Jackson, Mississippi

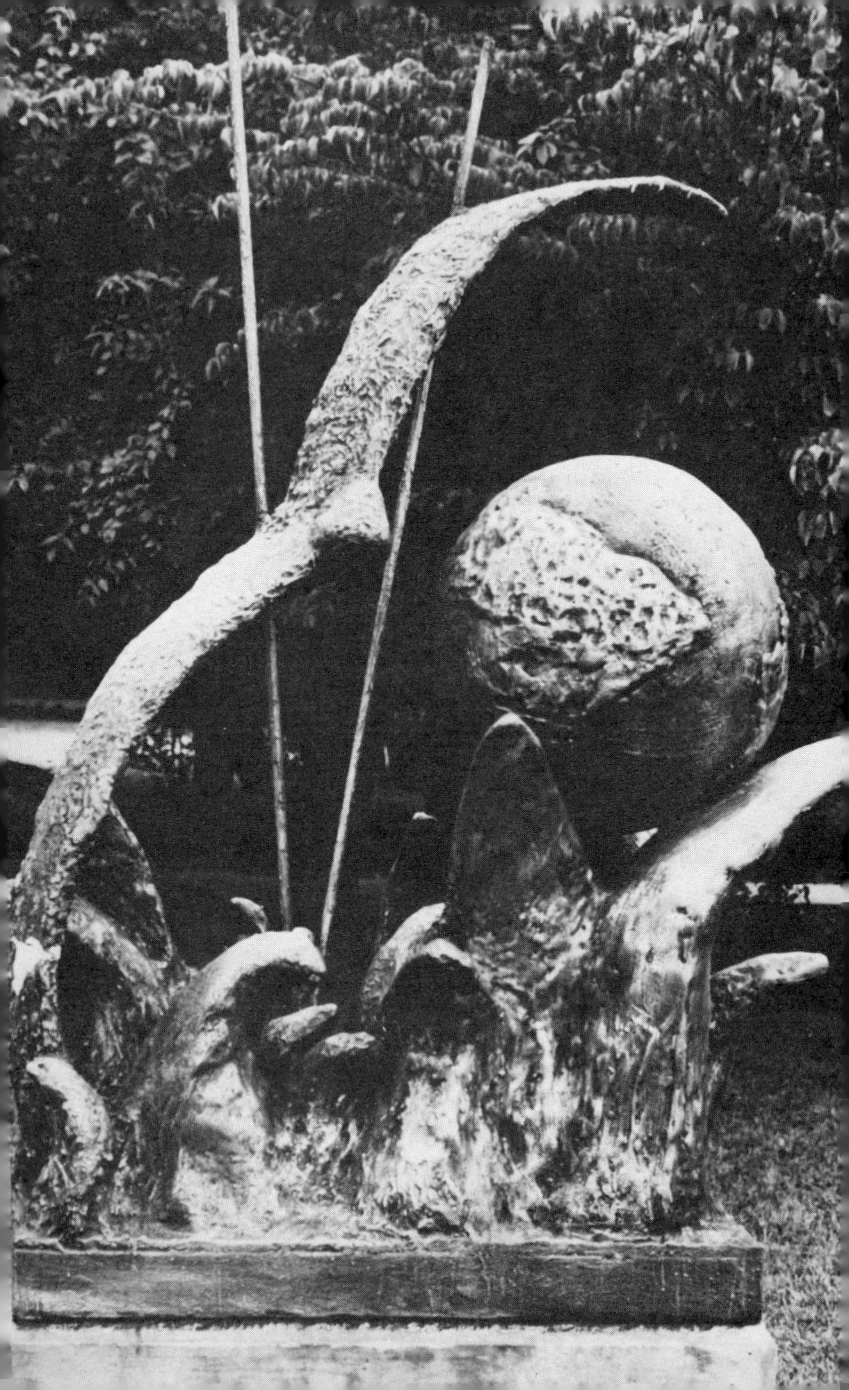

Creation • September 29–October 5

September 29

"Has not one God created us?" (Mal. 2:10a, RSV.)

In his infinite wisdom, God formed us and gave us our being. In his image we are alike, yet each a different person. His power created us with varied abilities. But to each of us he gave the ability to love. We thank him that this is so. In his wisdom, God formed no two stars in the heavens alike, no two flowers, no two birds, fish, animals, or creeping insects exactly alike. Scientists have found no two snowflakes, even, to be exactly the same.

God wants us to be happy in his beautiful world. For service, for personal relationships and for our delight, God has blessed us with five wonderful senses—touch, smell, taste, sight, and hearing.

We praise thee, Creator-Father!

TOUCH September 30

Touch is the first sense developed in the newborn infant. The touch of gentle hands provides comfort. The baby, cradled in loving arms, feels secure. It is in relation to others that we are most aware of the sense of touch. Deep emotions are expressed with a friendly handclasp, a pat on the back, a tender kiss, a warm embrace. We inflict pain when in rejection, prejudice, or rage we push or shove in our impatience.

Jesus touched those about him. Life flowed from him, even to the edge of his robe. He touched a dead child and life was restored. He touched the eyes of the blind and the eyes were opened. Our lives, too, can be so charged with the love of God that our touch will carry with it healing and blessing.

Smell   October 1

Perhaps the sense of smell is the one we think least about. It is, nonetheless, one of our richest blessings. It is an exquisite delight to step out of doors on a bright morning when the air is heavy with the fragrance of flowers—a lilac bush in bloom, honeysuckle draped along a fence, fruit trees blossoming in the garden.

Kitchen smells—the aroma of baking bread, roasting turkey, or the scent of vanilla from a cake in the oven—awaken slumbering memories and remind us of many happy family feasts. In contrast, we sense decay and pollution as poisonous gases fill the air and waters are rendered putrid by carelessness and greed.

Father, we thank thee for this beautiful world. Help us preserve it, we pray. *Amen.*

Taste   October 2

Taste is one of the most enjoyable of the senses. We are given this that we may enjoy the foods of the earth from the simplest to the most exotic. (But we were also given reason, so that we may control our appetites.) As we taste and enjoy food from other lands, we realize that God has spread his blessings throughout the world.

Food was used to glorify God when Jesus blessed a boy's meager lunch and fed five thousand hungry people. We partake of the suffering of our Lord when we eat the broken bread and drink from the communion cup. We share ourselves when we break bread with strangers and make them one with us in fellowship. We accept the admonition of Jesus, who said to Peter in utter tenderness, "Feed my lambs" (John 21:15b, RSV).

SIGHT — October 3

Sight is perhaps our richest blessing. With it we behold the wonders of God's creation. We also see people around us who are poor, afflicted, discriminated against, hungry, and even starving. If we see them as Jesus did, we are moved with compassion.

When we travel, we see outreach money at work and we feel the need for deeper involvement both at home and abroad. In Africa we see a village church, with a local pastor preaching and teaching. In Southeast Asia, we see, near a Buddhist temple, a Christian hospital bringing hope and healing to many. We see schools, homes for children and aging, and Christian service centers.

Dear Father, help us see as Jesus did so that we are moved with compassion and become involved. *Amen.*

HEARING — October 4

God gave us ears that we might hear. To miss the sound of music, the voices of children at play, or the singing of birds in early morning would be loss, indeed. But to miss hearing the voice of one who cries out in need, in frustration, in despair—this is a far greater loss, for such a voice is a call to service.

We must listen to one another in our own homes, to our companions and to our children, even when they speak in protest. We should hear the voices of youth who are trying to tell us that they, too, are searching for life's meaning. In meeting together, we need to listen to those with whom we disagree. We might learn something of great value. God means for us to listen to one another.

Father, help us be quiet enough to hear you speak. *Amen.*

CREATIVITY			October 5

We offer joyous praise this day for all our rich blessings. As we look back across a century, we give thanks for our sisters who, by their faith and vision, laid a lasting foundation upon which Christian Women's Fellowship is still building. With limited resources, they showed real creativity. Today, in a widened area of service some among us have great gifts. They use their skills to organize, to write and to speak, bringing inspiration and blessing to many. Others express their gifts of creativity in quiet ways. Alone and in groups they are busy at many tasks. As we all move forward in love and Christian fellowship, may our faith be deepened, our vision clarified, and our creativity enlarged.

Ruth Morris Graham, Claremont, California

Keeping Things in Perspective ● October 6−12

FAMILIES IN PERSPECTIVE			October 6

Luke 8:19−21; Eph. 5:21−33

Our love for husbands, children, parents—members of our family—is deeper than all other human ties. But we seek a balance here, too. God, our Creator, authored these family relationships as a definite plan for procreation and as a basic unit to reflect his love.

The love we feel for members of our family, no matter how deep and sincere, is at the same time an extension of our love of God. We respond to God by responding to people. True love helps each participant grow and mature through interaction with another. God has planned this to bring a fuller knowledge of himself into our world.

We love God first; then he gives us the privilege of expressing love to another person. We see the purpose of families as we mature in response to God's love.

RELIGION IN PERSPECTIVE

October 7

Josh. 23:1—16

Religion is not the practice of certain rules and rituals, not the meeting together in organized groups for formal exercises. Many mistake these observances for religion. We get so bogged down in the surface signs of faith that we lose all contact with real religion.

We can make a fetish out of religious practices, assume pompous attitudes of piety, and never live a day of truly religious life. Such excesses do much harm and drive people away from God.

Our religion should be concerned with the whole sum of our existence as a creation of God. Our total understanding and response to God's will for us as individuals make up a religious life. Our thoughts and actions *are* our religion. We cannot separate what we think from what we are.

CAREERS IN PERSPECTIVE

October 8

Phil. 4:1—13

Our natural abilities and interests should lead us to choose suitable vocations. Several choices are usually open to each of us. The prime consideration should be not the renumeration or acclaim we receive but the chance the work offers for advancing Christ's kingdom.

Then we need to keep in perspective the amount of time devoted to a career. We could fall into the trap of giving every waking hour to our work, excluding all thoughts of others and God. We should give the employer a fair return for compensation received, but the first business of our lives should be to preach Christ in word and in action.

If we make exemplifying Christ our goal, then a career will assume its rightful place in our lives.

Material Things in Perspective — October 9
Mark 10:17–22; 12:13–17

The love of money, fine cars, homes, clothes, expensive toys and trinkets can sometimes become the ruling force in our lives. It is not wrong to have great riches if they are used wisely, but we cannot justify our wealth just by giving to the less fortunate and needy. Our attitude is what counts and on it we will be judged. We should share for the love of God, not to appease God.

If our financial resources are small, we are also judged by our attitude. The way in which our modest funds are spent can be a Christian witness. We should not squander money on frivolities, leaving nothing to share with others. A Christ-like attitude toward life can be reflected in our use of money.

Use of Time in Perspective — October 10
Mark 3:1–6

Time is a gift to be used wisely. We are constrained to do things for the good of other people and so exemplify the life of Christ. All our actions should be directed toward this end. Many activities and interests compete for our time but we need to set priorities and do the things that advance the kingdom of God.

Making choices between two good things is difficult but such choices can strengthen us. A busy person will always accomplish more and be able to carry on more worthwhile projects by organizing her time, choosing which jobs are most important and quickly getting them done. Spending time worrying about having too much to do steals time from God and destroys our effectiveness.

We must be aware of responsibility. We must set priorities. We must act.

Keeping Our Bodies in Perspective October 11
Rom. 12:1-2; 1 Cor. 6:12-20; 10:13-31

Many women have added extra pounds to their physical bodies, thereby becoming miserable, irascible, and ineffective. Blaming heredity and doctors' ineptness cripples the soul and denies it a chance to function well. The body is the temple of God and its functions must be in perspective and in balance.

Stripping away excuses and pretenses, a woman can actually give God glory for the temptation of food. A person should accept this problem, not as a weakness but as an opportunity for character growth. Every severe temptation is accompanied by extra discipline to face the temptation.

A disciplined life moves us from physical priorities to spiritual revelation.

Emotions in Perspective October 12
Mark 11:15-19

Emotions are the necessary catalysts that move the world. But emotions in the wrong degree can cripple a person and stop all growth and development. We need emotion to the right degree to spur us into action.

Righteous indignation has a definite function in the affairs of people. We need to have the courage to change things that are unjust or evil. This is a healthy use of emotion. Anger can channel all a person's energy and determination to correct some wrong. But too much anger can harm a person. Love in correct proportions can change the world. Too much love changes into something that destroys.

Let us control emotions with judgment and discretion.

Ida Spitz Swindell, Charleston, South Carolina

Spiritual Availability • October 13–19

DETOUR INTO JOY October 13

When I went off with definite dreams to college from my little home town, I didn't expect my career in Christian education to be cut short by marriage, nor my robust husband to contract bulbar polio only four months after those vows about "in sickness and in health."

Life is full of rough detours as well as unexpected joys. Not a single line in the New Testament promises that because we're Christians we are immune to accidents, sickness, or hardship. Faith doesn't remove us from life. It simply makes us big enough to face whatever comes.

Through the years, the meaning of Paul's words has grown more precious: "We know that in everything God works for good with those who love him" (Rom. 8:28a, RSV).

FREEDOM TO CHOOSE COMMITMENT October 14

Everyone is made up of the sum total of personal commitments. Even in escaping responsibility, we can be enslaved by the need to flee and by the ways chosen to escape. The only freedom that means anything is the liberty to decide what we will do with our hours and resources. Even though God has deep, infinite hopes for how we will use our years, he gives us freedom to choose for ourselves.

Like an earthly parent, God feels disappointment and pain when we are estranged from him. He knows that his children are shaped by the things they love but he loves us too much to make puppets of us. Therefore he gives us a precious but dangerous gift—freedom. That is why he is overjoyed by our free and loving choice of him as Lord.

Dear Father, give me the courage to choose the best. *Amen.*

RESTLESS PATIENCE
October 15

I nag my teen-age son about how important it is to drive his car patiently. Hurried, anxious driving causes many accidents. Then I examine my soul and recognize my own impatience when things don't happen as I think they should. I am strengthened by remembering that even the early Christians had their capacity for enduring frustration tested daily. To them, Paul wrote this description of a process we can testify happens in us, too—"Suffering produces endurance, and endurance produces character, and character produces hope" (Rom. 5:3b—4, RSV). "If we hope for what we do not see," he explains, "we wait for it with patience" (Rom. 8:25, RSV). Patience—not indifference! We work but we also know how to wait with trust for our work to ripen.

DON'T CARE CARELESSLY
October 16

We have strong instincts to heal the wounds of others. Whenever we know of a problem situation in a friend's life or within a struggling organization, we feel impelled to help. But we need solitude and inner peace in which our private turmoil can be stilled before we are best equipped to nurture others.

We won't find inner peace by looking longingly toward the past, nor dreaming of a rosy future. We need to discover the magic of the present—the here and now—to taste it, enjoy it, and find in it the very presence of Christ who made us his caring people.

Then, tapped into his infinite store of grace, patience, hope, energy, and beauty, we find ourselves able to help others, as we are backed by a power beyond our own.

SEEING INVISIBLE HOPE — October 17

Often, even when we cannot explain why, despair possesses us. I don't know very many real, loving persons whom despair doesn't visit sometimes. Yet hope is available to those who believe God's promise that "we have been born anew to a living hope . . ." (1 Peter 1:3b, RSV).

God makes it possible for us to receive hope from others in the unseen grace and strength that come from those we love. Giving birth to a baby is thrilling—a new creation and a new hope. Watching someone walk down the church aisle to join his or her life to the congregation is a joy to all because it is full of hope. Seeing one's children accept new responsibility is a source of hope for the future. All around us are great evidences of God's Spirit at work, inspiring hope in those who can see.

MAKING LOVE RELIGIOUSLY — October 18

Those who have been loved can understand why so many people are hungry for love. It is strange that we do not seek more thoughtful ways to express our love to others. Our instinct to do this is probably a prompting by the Holy Spirit, because the Spirit represents a Christ who cared so much he gave his life for us. We can understand why one New Testament writer appealed to the early church: "Dear friends! Let us love one another, because love comes from God" (1 John 4:7a, TEV).

To obey the prompting of God's Spirit may mean we will have to revise our busy schedules enough to be more available to love others and express our concern for them, even if we risk being hurt as Christ was hurt.

Dear Father, teach me to love as you love. *Amen.*

A Plea to One Who Always Hears   October 19

Our heavenly Father, in all we do may we offer simple and sincere prayers, for you are always available to the earnest heart. In our crowded lives, we often feel that joy is stolen from us too easily. Since we are exposed daily to fear and doubt, to weariness and impatience, keep our tempers from wearing so thin that we are robbed of peace of mind. When skies are gray, help us remember that the sun of your Spirit shines behind them and we can feel its warmth through them. We are glad for the confidence in our hearts that you are with us in times of joy and pain. In every circumstance, even in our greatest weakness, your unchanging strength is available to us. In the name of Jesus Christ. *Amen.*

Leona V. Kechel, Portland, Oregon

Commitment • October 20−26

October 20

Suggested Reading: "Our Ultimate Concern," in *The New Being*, by Paul Tillich.

Every person is committed to something. Everyone of us gives herself to something. We invest our lives in that which we value. Something holds us up and gives our lives meaning. Something is our goal.

To what am I committed? To what do I give myself? What is it that uses my energy? How do I spend my time, my money, my talents, my resources? Do I use my energy in spinning my wheels? Do I reach the end of the day and feel that I have not really given myself to anything? Do I feel that I am no closer to the goal of my life than I was a week ago, a month ago, a year ago? To what can I give myself that will put my life together?

COMMITTED TO GOD   October 21

Suggested Reading: *Living Without God Before God*, by David O. Woodyard.

The Christian is the human being committed to God. Loving God with heart, mind, soul, strength —everything—is at the core of the life of the Christian. The things we decide to do as Christians are those that help us to love God more perfectly.

Nothing is more important to us than discovering God in the events of living. We discover God is *beyond* everything we think or do. Yet he is *in* them. He is greater than our highest thought. Yet he is closer than our thoughts.

God is a mystery, revealed and yet hidden, known and unknown. In our commitment to that mystery we find the meaning for our lives.

COMMITTED TO NEIGHBOR   October 22

Suggested Reading: *On Caring*, by Milton Mayeroff

The Christian is the human being committed to the love of neighbor. Love of neighbor is tied up irrevocably with love of God. No one, not even a Christian, can love God if he does not at the same time care about his neighbor. Love of neighbor must go beyond the one from whom we borrow sugar.

Our love of neighbor must cause us to go out of our way to see that the person neglected by social structures is no longer shut off from the love of God. We must be those who care about the left-out ones. We will not be forgiven if we do not stretch our imaginations and our sight to see our neighbor as the one the world has forgotten.

COMMITTED TO COMMUNITY   October 23

Suggested Reading: "The Situation of Life in Christ," in *Life in Christ*, by Norman Pittinger.

The Christian is the human being committed to creating community. It's clear that we cannot live by ourselves. We have learned that we depend on each other. We need other people to help us discover our world and the meaning of our lives. We need to love; we need to be loved. We cannot fulfill these needs unless we build strong, intimate communities where we trust and are trusted, where we love and are loved.

The church is such a community. The church is that body of people committed to creating a community where no one is a stranger. In the church, persons can make concrete their commitment to loving God and neighbor.

COMMITTED TO INTEGRITY   October 24

Suggested Reading: *Morality and Beyond*, by Paul Tillich.

The Christian is the human being committed to integrity. She acts out what she says. She acts in the same manner in which she speaks. There is no noticeable difference between what she says and what she does. Her actions are the drama of her words. She becomes to others the living word. In her the gospel has become reality. She does not only talk of love; she loves. She does not only talk about reconciliation; she knocks on the door and encounters the other person. She does not only pray for the hungry; she feeds them. The world will not believe us when we say we love God and neighbor if we have not been love in flesh. Our words become noise unless we offer our bodies as instruments of love.

COMMITTED TO JESUS, THE CHRIST — October 25

Suggested Reading: *In Christ's Place*, by Ronald Osborn.

To be Christian is to be a human being committed to following Jesus Christ. Commitment to Jesus Christ means finding in his life and death a way of relating to the world. That way is looking at the world through the eyes of the one who has seen God and has shown us what God is like. That way is the way of servant. We certainly cannot expect to do less than the Lord of our lives. His life judges our life. His love judges our love. We find in him the meaning of being a person, a human being committed to God. We, who use his name, must also use his way of living. His God must be our God. His mission must be our mission. Committed to him, we find over and over again the new life promised in the Easter event.

COMMITTED TO THE CROSS — October 26

Suggested Reading: "Death," in *The Last Things in a Process Perspective*, by Wm. Norman Pittenger.

The Christian is the human being committed to carrying her own cross. She is the one who gets out of the spectator's chair and moves into the arena of human hurt. She is the one who gets in under the cross and helps carry the burden. She is the one who walks beside and not behind or in front of her neighbor. She is the one who listens and responds to the cries of the prostitute, the drunk, the lost, the lonely, the uninspired, the bored, the hungry, the wealthy, the poor.

The cross is the eternal sign of the suffering of humankind and the cruelty of humankind. It is also the sign of the love of God which goes beyond our understanding.

Becky Bunton, Stilesville, Indiana

Looking to the Future • October 27−31

October 27

One summer, while I was a seminary student, I was invited to preach at a church near my hometown. The people welcomed me graciously and were interested in my plans to enter the ministry. One well-meaning elder, rather surprised and not knowing quite what to do with my decision to be a minister, said pleasantly, "Well, that's nice. I suppose when there's a shortage of ministers, women are needed."

I believe the future for women in the church will be determined in part by our ability to claim for ourselves the validity of our own calling. We are not leaders and churchwomen by default—because someone else refused the job. We must work with our brothers and not in their places, sharing a common mission and responsibility.

Lord, help us claim boldly our calling as persons. *Amen.*

October 28

Early in my professional ministry I was surprised to discover an unsuspected obstacle—my own internalized prejudice. Standing firm in my conviction for legitimate ministry by women in the face of criticism has been challenging, if sometimes frustrating. The real enemy whom I have come to know, however, is the one inside myself. At times I have believed that I was less adequate than my male colleagues and have doubted my own strength, shrinking back and failing to use my potential. As often I have felt the opposite pressure to overcompensate and prove myself as supercompetent. Either extreme is unhappy. But whatever I may think others expect from me, it is my own self-image that causes me to act and that, in the end, will give me both the most pain and the ultimate joy.

October 29

On a popular television show, a TV doctor was dealing with the problem of overweight. The patient, whose struggles were very real to those of us who have ever tried to lose weight, was told, "To stay with the hard discipline of a diet, you really have to like yourself."

The future of women, the church, and even the human race depends on our ability to like ourselves deeply. The Scriptures teach us to love our neighbor as ourself. Loving ourself makes it possible for us to love our neighbor. The church and the world will be greatly enriched by people who learn to act out of personal freedom and integrity because they feel themselves to be of worth.

Lord, thank you for loving me; help me love myself and, therefore, others. *Amen.*

October 30

Acts 11:1—18

This account of the struggle of Jews to accept Gentiles is a powerful message for contemporary church and society. God was seen to have given the same gift of spiritual baptism to the Gentiles as he had given to the Jews. When the penetrating question was asked, "Who was I that I could withstand God?" (Acts 11:17b, RSV), they rejoiced in God and accepted the Gentiles.

The Spirit is alive in the world, breaking through every area of life to make all things new. There can be no second-class citizens in the kingdom of God. The crucial question for the church is whether we will withstand God by rigidly organizing persons according to outdated stereotypes, thus limiting the leading of the Spirit among us.

Lord, help us accept new life. *Amen.*

October 31

Proverbs 3:17

Gracious God, Mother/Father of all creation,
  enfold us in your peace;
    dwell among us as Brother/Sister;
      and bind us together in pleasantness.
We confess to you that we are not all that we should be.
  We have dealt with you so as to confine your movement;
    we have scorned each other and acted as strangers;
    we have not known how to love ourselves.
Deliver us from the confines of our own narrow ways;
  enrich us with the diversity of your creation;
    fill us with the hope of love's incarnation;
      send us by your Holy Spirit into all the world
        to declare your Presence and share our humanness. *Amen.*

Claudia Ewing Grant, Indianapolis, Indiana

Eternal, Yet Always New

"Shall the sisters speak?" "Do the Christian scriptures authorize females to lead in prayer in the meetings of the church for worship?" One hundred years ago, the answer was an almost unanimous No! But this did not stifle the prayer life of Christian women. For many, the hard life of the pioneer was the order of the day and they well knew that prayer had seen them through many difficult occasions. In small prayer meetings of the "sisters," in family prayer circles and in private devotional life these women of 100 years ago rose to majestic spiritual heights, where they received power to walk in new paths and undertake new tasks.

It is good that in our celebration of the one hundredth anniversary of the Christian Woman's Board of Missions we have made special preparation for daily spiritual nourishment. In days when our horizons and opportunities have broadened beyond anything that could have been imagined by the women of 1874, we dare not forget that our strength is sustained not only by our relationships with each other and in groups but also in time spent in private meditation and communion with God.

Christian women of each generation listen and respond to God's word as it is spoken to them in their times. His word is eternal, yet somehow always new, with accents and emphasis appropriate for *this* day.

Helen F. Spaulding, Indianapolis, Indiana

Index of Authors

Adams, Elaine G.	169–172
Austin, Kathleen Bailey	72–76
Barnes, Joyce	54–57
Broadus, Catherine	69–72
Bunton, Becky	199–202
Burchill, Eleanor Meyers	124–128
Clark, Peggy Owen	154–157
Craddock, Fran	65–68
Darling, Ethel	57–60
Dixon, Virginia	166–169
Doty, Estella	144–147
Draper, Dean	87–90
Evans, Edith R.	114–117
France, Dorothy D.	106–110
Fulton, Ivy	50–53
Gordon, Jean	13–16
Graham, Ruth Morris	189–192
Grant, Claudia Ewing	203–205
Hoak, Johanna	32–35
Hogan, Bernice	91–94
Howlett, Lois	39–43
Hubbard, Hannah B.	47–50
Hubbell, Mrs. T. V.	80–83
Jarman, Ginger Brittain	27–31
Kechel, Leona V.	196–199
Kuss, Eleanor S.	102–105
Landry, Judith	98–102
Leland, Joyce	121–124
Massay, Alice	20–23
McGowan, Anice	84–87
Meece, Georgia	159–162
Meisburg, Gladys H.	184–187
Metcalf, Jackie	17–20
Moseley, Carol Ann	35–38
Park, Willetta	117–120
Pew, Lois Jean	173–177

Pouncy, Eunell	110–113
Pratt, Louise	162–165
Reed, Virgi	136–139
Richards, Dorothy A.	147–150
Rowand, Mary Louise	94–97
Rush, Jeanne	181–184
Schooler, Alma	132–135
Spaulding, Helen F.	206
Stegall, Kay	24–27
Swindell, Ida Spitz	192–195
Taylor, Marilyn	151–154
Trout, Jessie M.	7–8
VanBoskirk, Irene	77–80
Vanderkolk, Jody	129–132
Velazquez, Joyce	61–65
Warren, Karen	139–143
Westbrook, Bertha	177–180
Woolcock, Mertie	43–46
Wyker, Mossie Allman	11–13